S0-BJG-251

SCRIPTURE TODAY

Scripture Today
Handling the Word Rightly

G. Allen Fleece Library
Columbia International University
Columbia, SC 29203

The Eleventh National Conference
of Trinity Institute

Durstan R McDonald, Editor

MOREHOUSE-BARLOW CO., INC.
Wilton, Connecticut

Columbia International University
Columbia SC 29203

Copyright © 1980 Trinity Institute
All rights reserved

MOREHOUSE-BARLOW CO., INC.
78 Danbury Road
Wilton, CT 06897

ISBN 0-8192-1271-7

Library of Congress Catalogue Card No. 80-81100

Printed in the United States of America

Other Books From Trinity Institute

The Future of the Christian Church
Arthur Michael Ramsey
Leon-Joseph Suenens

The Charismatic Christ
Arthur Michael Ramsey
Robert E. Terwilliger
A. MacDonald Allchin

Come Holy Spirit
Arthur Michael Ramsey
Robert E. Terwilliger

The Myth/Truth of God Incarnate
Don Cupitt
John Macquarrie
Michael Marshall
Dennis Nineham
Richard A. Norris, Jr.
Roy I. Sano
Jon Sobrino

Contents

Preface

The Christian Church has always understood Holy Scripture to be normative for its faith and practice. For most American Christians the simplest way to affirm the centrality of Scriptures is to affirm that the Bible is the Word of God. Just as Luther, Calvin, Zwingli and The Council of Trent differed on what it means to rely on Scripture, so do contemporary Christians. Just as different views of Scripture led to different social-political arrangements in Switzerland, Germany, and Rome, so today different ways of reading Scripture lead to different conclusions about the family and the Christian's relationship to the government. Since Christians disagree in good faith about almost any and every passage of Scripture, any thoughtful person must have some good reason not to become cynical about reading the Scriptures. If good and faithful people answer so differently the question, "What does this passage say to us," how can we believe that we are doing anything more than using Scripture to support our own position?

For some the way out of the dilemma has been to appeal to the inerrancy of Holy Writ. The Anglican tradition has consistently eschewed such an appeal as one of the two enduring forms of human weakness and spiritual bankruptcy. Any nervous anxiety that attempts to freeze God's Word in the written text, ignoring the changing meaning of the words in changing times, must be rejected. On the other hand, equally disastrous are the attempts of those who would let the mind of "modern man" determine what we can believe and assert. The latter falls into the trap of allowing the culture alone to determine our faith, whereas the former freezes the Word into a previous culture. Both perceive the truth in what they assert positively, and err in their denials. The "fundamentalist" understands that there is a self-communi-

cation of God given in the person of Jesus and conveyed to us in
Scripture that transcends, and often judges, our culture and our
uncritical assumptions. The "modernist" understands that the
meaning of any communication is, in part, determined by the
context and that the meaning of a passage of Scripture *for us*
will be determined, in part, by the conditions of *our* world.

Before we begin to ask what any specific passage of Scripture
is saying to us today, we must have a clear understanding of the
hermeneutical issues involved. *How* we think Scripture is to be
interpreted will affect what we will find in any given passage.
Before asking about Scripture's teaching about marriage, divorce,
wealth, abortion, salvation, and the like, we must reflect on how
to avoid liberal and conservative forms of rationalization alike.

The National Conference at which these essays formed the
formal addresses also included six workshops on the meaning of
key Scriptural passages for the church today. Since the informality
of these sessions precluded their publication in this volume, the
reader might first consider one or two before going further. The
passages are Genesis 1:27, Ecclesiastes 6, Matthew 5:39-42,
Luke 16:1-9, Ephesians 5:21-33, Revelation 19.

In his keynote sermon O.C. Edwards reminds us of the power
of Scripture as inspired by God. Reviewing key moments in the
life of the church, he suggests that every renewal movement had
its point of departure in a new interpretation of Scripture. Far
from being a deficiency, the very capacity of the Bible to illuminate situations for what is meant by the doctrine demonstrates
that the Bible is the inspired word. What the church needs, then,
more than anything else is restored confidence in the power of
the written word to accomplish God's purpose in new contexts
with new meanings. And that, for all of us, means that reading
Scripture is "a very risky business."

Frederick Borsch locates the task as moving beyond the traps
of three well established approaches to the interpretation of the
Bible. Historically, western Catholicism has viewed the institutional church as the interpreter of Scripture. The rise of the
historical-critical method has to a large extent replaced older
understandings of the interpretive authority of the magisterium.

For many in the Protestant tradition, Scripture is interpreted through the individual's experience and reason, i.e. by the direct reading of the believer in light of his or her own life. It is at this point that the problem of an arbitrarily subjective reading of the Bible is more severe. An alternative is to deny that any interpretation is necessary, in principal. That human reason and experience are to be judged by Scripture, not vice-versa, is the claim of those who assert the fundementalist doctrine of plenary inspiration.

To Borsch, each of these approaches results in a mis-hearing and mis-handling of Scripture. Instead, he argues, what is needed is a "hermeneutic of engagement" which will include three movements: hearing Scripture, interpreting it, and acting upon it. Only by attending to the narrative quality of Scripture and the many different uses of language in Scripture will we be able to grasp the power of the Bible to "lure us toward the frontier of the kingdom and the mystery of new possibilities for life in relationship with God." In his article, David Tracy points also to the importance of the different kinds of language within Scripture as leading to different types of spirituality, each authentically Christian.

Jim Wallis' discussion of "Pentecostal economics" is a specific example of attempting what Borsch proposes, i.e. a fundamental engagement with the Bible. Arguing that Scripture must always be read in the historical context of the reader, he maintains that American Christians must remember one key fact of the world today, namely, that the world's people are poor and the church in our country is rich. This fact and Jesus' emphatic teaching about wealth affects everything else. He sees the fundamental issues as trust in God and where we find our security. In proposing a Pentecostal economics in which the primitive church experienced the power of the Spirit's presence as impelling them into a new life together and into new economic arrangements, he cuts through the usual dichotomy between issues of justice or economics and personal spirituality. He thinks the meaning of Scripture is clear if we will only face the facts of life today and the clear teaching of Jesus.

Peggy Way steps back to suggest to clergy, and by implication to all Christians who minister to friends or others, that they often undervalue their own worth and contributions. The influence of the therapeutic model for understanding life and ministering to others has undercut our own sense of worth as Holy People, called by God. The therapeutic model must be replaced by an ecclesiastical model in which holiness is at the heart of human life. The priestly role of the people of God is focused on the interpretation of historical existence with a specific person. The priest or minister has a special task and a distinctive function in helping others to answer what it means to live on this side of the promised land. Only if this is understood, only if one is engaged in pastoral hermeneutics, she argues, only then will Scripture have an essential role in a ministry that includes and transcends the purely therapeutic.

Just as Peggy Way takes the insights of therapeutic knowledge to move into a consideration of the pastoral task, so too David Tracy utilizes the insights of contemporary literary critism and philosophical hermeneutics to develop a typology of two contrasting modes of spirituality in the New Testament. He analyzes the structure of language used by Paul to demonstrate that in itself it contains the dialectic of contradiction with the world, while he sees the linguistic structure of the Johannine writings as meditational. In the first case, we have a spirituality based on the Cross, the irreducible paradox and contradiction between God's ways and ours. The Gospel of John, on the other hand, is thoroughly incarnational and lends itself to a mystical perception of the co-inherence of all things in God. Each writer includes both dimensions, of course, but the structure of the narrative and the linguistic system of each establishes radically different modes of spirituality. To see each at the heart of the New Testament is not only to affirm that they are complementary, but also to understand why different people gravitate so consistently to different parts of the New Testament.

Any faithful response to Scriptures will have to do justice both to the diversity of interpretations of Scripture and the power of the Bible to break us out of our prejudices and favorite convictions. There is no going back on the historical-critical method, our own experiences, or the use of reason to find the Word of God speaking to our contemporary situation. On this the writers agree, but more important, they point us to ways in which we can discern the Word of the Lord, if we will be willing to have ears that hear and eyes that see.

Durstan R McDonald

The Living Word

O. C. Edwards*

When most of us think of the conversion of St. Paul, we think of it first and foremost as a religious experience. That is very natural. Revivalism has been the most distinctive characteristic of American Christianity during most of our history. Then, when revivalism began to lose some of its hold on American consciousness, psychology was waiting right there to fill the vacuum. And now that evangelism has again become a respectable word among Episcopalians we are pleased to be able to point to a New Testament example of what happens when it occurs successfully.

It is not surprising that we should instinctively interpret Paul's conversion as a religious experience. St. Luke certainly provided evidence for such an interpretation by his report of what we would call the psychosomatic aspects of this event: the flash of light, the force that threw Paul to the ground, the voice from heaven, the blindness and fasting that followed.

Yet we seldom ask what Paul was converted *from* and what he was converted *to.* When we think of anyone else's conversion we normally think of a conversion from sin to righteousness, but where do we find evidence that Paul was a sinner before his conversion? He tells us in his own account of this event that he

*The Very Rev. O. C. Edwards is President and Dean of Seabury-Western Theological Seminary. A New Testament and Patristics scholar, he is the author or co-author of several books, including THE BIBLE FOR TODAY'S CHURCH, *and co-editor of* A FAITHFUL CHURCH: ISSUES IN THE HISTORY OF CATECHESIS, *to be published early in 1981 by Morehouse-Barlow Co. This article formed the basis of the opening sermon at the Conference.*

"advanced in Judaism beyond many of [his] own age among [his] people, so extremely zealous was [he] for the traditions of [his] fathers" (Gal. 1:14). True, he does seem to have some remorse for having persecuted Christians before he became one, but we see little in him that is guilt-ridden. In fact, it is just the opposite: Paul is notorious for his good opinion of himself. It is true that *we* are accustomed to think of pride as the deadliest of sins and can say that what endangered Paul the Pharisee was his very awareness of keeping the law so scrupulously, but where in all of his writings do we find Paul saying that?

Another interpretation of his conversion could be that it was from Judaism to Christianity. But where do we find Paul saying that he was no longer a Jew? Christianity did not become a religion that was clearly distinguishable from Judaism until after the destruction of Jerusalem in 70 A.D., some six to ten years after Paul's death. The complete separation was not accomplished until about 90 A.D. when the rabbis at Jamnia wrote into the synagogue service things that no Christian could say. Thus it is anachronistic to say that Paul was converted from one religion to another. Rather he changed his membership from one reform movement within Judaism to another; he left the party that thought the followers of Jesus should be persecuted and joined the party that believed Jesus to be the messiah.

Krister Stendahl, the Swedish New Testament scholar and Dean of Harvard Divinity School, has indeed offered cogent argument for the thesis that we should not speak of St. Paul's *conversion* but should speak instead of his *call.* Certainly the emphasis in all three accounts of this event in Acts is on the work God had in store for Paul that he revealed to him there on the Damascus road. In the version that was the lesson for the Conference service we heard that call in these words:

> I have appeared to you for this purpose, to appoint you to serve and bear witness to the . . . Gentiles—to whom I send you to open their eyes, that they may turn from darkness to light and from the power of Satan to God, and that they may receive forgiveness of sins and a place among those who are sanctified by faith in me (Acts 26:16-18).

And, while Paul's own account of this event in Galatians does not agree entirely with Acts about what happened, it does confirm this one point that Paul received his vocation to be the apostle to the gentiles at that moment. Paul calls the event "a revelation of Jesus Christ" and goes on to say:

> He who set me apart before I was born, and had called me through his grace, was pleased to reveal his Son to me, in order that I might preach him among the Gentiles.

Stendahl correctly points out the close parallel between Paul's description of this event and the accounts that Old Testament prophets give of their calls. I would, however, want to modify Stendahl's thesis to this extent: at the time that Paul received his call he was also converted to belief in the messiahship of Jesus. Thus there are elements of both conversion and call in this event, but the conversion had to take place before the call could be heard.

The conversion to belief in the messiahship of Jesus also involved conversion from one way of understanding the Torah to another. Previously, Paul had regarded the Torah as the full statement of God's will for his people. Obeying it was the means by which one came to be accepted by God as righteous. Now, though, he was to come to a different understanding. God had promised to bless all nations of the world through Abraham. The law was not given to Moses until 430 years after the promise to Abraham. This meant that the law was not the means by which the promise would be kept. The promise would be kept instead through Jesus, the seed of Abraham. The law had a much humbler role: to keep Israel in line until the fulfillment of the promise in Jesus. As Stendahl paraphrases it, Paul says that the law "came as a harsh baby sitter to see to it that the children of Israel did not raid the refrigerator before the great party at which the Gentiles should also be present."

All of the foregoing has been by way of preface to the main point I wish to make: the conversion of St. Paul was, among other things, a conversion from reading the Bible one way to reading it another way. That statement is the basis for another: most of the great renewal movements in the history of the church have grown out of new insights into the meaning of the Bible. To comprehend this is to make contact with the theme of this

Eleventh National Conference of Trinity Institute, "Scripture Today: Handling the Word Rightly."

One thing that should be obvious about renewal movements that have had their point of departure from new interpretations of scripture is that they were *new* interpretations, often not what the sacred writer had in mind at all. For instance, a self-tormented Luther felt that all of his works of devotion as a monk were really inadequate to meet the demands of God until he was convinced by Paul that he did not have to earn God's approval. Yet Paul himself had no such doubts when he was still a Pharisee. Indeed, he tells us how well he did in observing the Torah. The self doubts of Luther were a product of what Stendahl calls "the introspective conscience of the West," something that did not even get a start until St. Augustine.

It should not surprise us that later generations have not always had an historical understanding of the biblical passages that inspired their renewal movements. When biblical traditions were re-appropriated within the canon itself, we find that they were usually understood in ways different from what was originally intended. This different understanding is shown in the different use to which a passage was put in different books. The gospel here under consideration is a case in point. Matthew, in Jesus' words to the Twelve as he sends them out on a mission in a final effort to beat the eschatological clock that is running out, includes these warnings that those who publish the good news of salvation in Jesus will be like sheep in the middle of a wolf pack. The parts of this discourse that appear in Mark are included in his Little Apocalypse in chapter 13. Luke has some of this material in the Marcan location but part of the rest is in one of the many speeches Jesus gives in the long travel narrative that makes up the middle third of his gospel. Käsemann has argued that these sayings did not originate in the ministry of Jesus himself but come from the post-resurrection church in Palestine before the fall of Jerusalem, a time when charismatic prophets were still engaged in trying to persuade Israelites outside Jerusalem to believe that the crucified Jesus was in reality the Messiah long expected by the Jews. In modern times, I have heard these same verses about not worrying beforehand what you are going to say by conservative evangelicals as arguments against sermon preparation. Part of what is involved in our claim that the Bible is inspired is its capacity to illuminate situations for which it was never envisioned. Obviously, some of these extensions are better than others, but our continuing return to the Bible as the fountain from which pours God's understanding of our situation demands that some such extensions be valid.

Indeed, that has been our experience. Many people can relate stories of how a chance reading of a certain passage has been like a bolt of lightning that brought into brilliant clarity the landscape of his or her existence at the time, a landscape that had been completely obscured by clouds and darkness before. To say this is to make no overwhelming claim. Anyone who has ever been involved in amateur theatricals is familiar with the way that a cast, when it finally has begun to memorize its lines, can find an apt quotation from the play for almost every situation that comes up. How much more can we expect the words that were inspired for the purpose to do the same.

I would like to share with you two of my own experiences of having passages from the Bible illuminate my existence. The first is rather general. There was a time when I was very conscious of being tempted and succumbing. During that period of my life I thought the story of the temptation of Adam and Eve in the Garden of Eden was incredibly insightful, holding up before me a mirror of my own responses. Later, as I aged and perhaps became protected by respectability from the contemplation of things that were liable to get me into too much hot water, the Eden story lost much of its appearance of relevance. In time, though, another story took its place, the story of the Ewe Lamb that Nathan told to David. I can empathize with David as he got caught up in the injustice done to the poor man and how his reaction was to want to punish the rich man for the terrible thing that he had done. Who was he, David cries out, so that I can see that he gets what he deserves. And Nathan turns to him and points his finger and says, "You are the man!" I seldom recognize my sins in advance anymore, but how bitter is the realization of what I have done when the consequences of my unthinking act are pointed out to me.

The other experience is much more specific. It has to do with one of the blackest moments of my life. It was during my first year of teaching at Nashotah House when I was still at work on my Ph.D. at the University of Chicago. I had my oral exams to take around the Christmas holidays and, for one reason or another, I thought they were a mere formality. You can imagine my dismay when I discovered that I was the only one who thought that. A new member of the faculty showed in vivid detail the inadequacy of the piece of work I had submitted as the basis for the exam. He showed this so clearly that even I realized it during the course of the exam, and the verdict that I had not only failed the exam but had even busted out of the program did not surprise me when it came. My gloom had no bottom. I assumed among other things that this failure meant that I was unqualified for my job and I waited for the Dean to tell me so. Days went by and he did not. It's the holidays, I said to myself by way of explanation. Finally, I could stand the suspense no longer and I sought him out. He was sorry about the result of the exam, but they posed no ultimate problem. He thought I had fitted in extraordinarily well and he was sure that I could get a degree somewhere. He wanted to thank me for the contribution that I was making to the community. You can imagine the mood in which I went to Evensong that night. The Psalm we sang was 126: ''When God turned again the captivity of Zion, then were we like unto them that dream. Then was our mouth filled with laughter and our tongue with joy.'' Talk about speaking to my condition! I knew exactly how the Psalmist felt.

The prophets had an understanding of the Word of God different from ours. Rather than thinking of everything that is contained in the Holy Scriptures, they thought of the word that God gave to them for the particular situation he wanted them to address—or, more precisely, he wanted to address through them. They knew that this word of his would accomplish exactly what it announced. Indeed, the prophecy and its fulfillment could be spoken of as the same event. God spoke and it was done. One of our new Prayer Book canticles quotes the Second Isaiah's beautiful statement of this point of view:

So is my word that goes forth from my mouth;
   it will not return to me empty;
But it will accomplish that which I have purposed,
   and prosper in that for which I have sent it.

What the church needs more than anything else is a restored confidence that what was true of the word to the prophet is also true of the written word; it will accomplish God's purpose for it, it will not return to him empty.

I am very aware when I say this that some of the loss of that expectation is the responsibility of those of us who have tried to teach biblical criticism in the seminaries. We thought that by use of the historical-critical method we could make the meaning of the Bible clearer. And we did. I do not think we can ever backtrack on this great tool for biblical interpretation. But in the process we lost sight of something. We treated the meaning of the Bible as something objective and historical. All we were interested in was the task of exegesis, showing what the sacred writer had wanted his first readers to understand. In doing so, we lost sight of the fact that the reason we study what the Bible *meant* is so that we can understand what it *means* today.

Not long ago the professors in the biblical field at Seabury-Western were meeting with those from Garrett-Evangelical, a United Methodist seminary across the street. One of the Garrett faculty was speaking of students and said, "You know, the trouble with these guys is that they read all these texts without the slightest suspicion that what they are about is themselves. They have no understanding at all that Bible reading is a very risky business. It is like walking through a mine field, never knowing when something is going to explode in your face. You take your life into your hands when you read this book." Another way of saying that is that "the Word of God is living and active and sharper than a two-edged sword." Of that there should be no doubt.

Ears That Hear and Do Not Hear: Fundamental Hearing of the Bible

Frederick H. Borsch*

"For whatever was written in former days was written for our instruction that by steadfastness and by encouragement of the scriptures we might have hope" (Romans 15:4). Even at the time Paul offered this counsel there was, however, uncertainty and controversy both with regard to which writings might be considered to be inspired by God and with respect to the character of their authority.[1] In a variety of forms and circumstances that controversy and uncertainty has continued throughout Christian history—sometimes rising to a high pitch of intensity, sometimes sounding in more muted and subtle tones. Our own times and culture are the context for a continuation of the debate but with these major differences: The Bible, while remaining important to the life of the churches, no longer plays a central role in society-at-large. In this respect we are more like the Christians of the first several generations than those of intervening centuries. Among those who do read and hear the Bible, however, there is, generally speaking, a keener consciousness of the fact that many contemporary concerns and questions are quite different from those of the people of the biblical cultures. The world views of biblical societies were so strikingly different from our own that reflective people today are aware of large gaps between our ways of perceiving and theirs.[2]

*Frederick H. Borsch, former Dean and Professor of New Testament at The Church Divinity School of the Pacific, is Dean of the Chapel, Princeton University. He has published a number of works in his field, including GOD'S PARABLE.

Uncertainty and controversy regarding the authority and use of the Bible are never far beneath the surface when contemporary Christians reflect on such matters as marriage and divorce, homosexuality, women in ministry, and how to build a more peaceful and just world order. In this article I wish to draw a sketch map of what I perceive to be the major approaches to the role of the scriptures today. It is my hope that this bit of cartography will be of assistance in raising significant questions which will be taken up in succeeding chapters of this book.

Influenced by the reformation but becoming much more pronounced during the nineteenth century, there emerged the strains of three major approaches to issues of the authority and interpretation of the Bible.

1. The essential authority of scripture passes from God through the institutional church, and the institutional church is the ultimate interpreter of scripture. This approach emphasizes the awareness that the Bible was formed by the community of faith.[3] It, therefore, belongs to the new Israel understood to be the church. Through divine guidance the leaders of the church—the church's magisterium (themselves guided by the long and, in fact, usually eclectic tradition of the church's interpretation of the Bible)—rightly understand scripture, hand it on, and interpret it to the people of today. Historically in western Catholicism the people's understanding of the message of the Bible has been formed, not so much directly through the reading of scripture, as indirectly through liturgy and ethical pronouncements.

2. Scripture is interpreted through the reason and experience of individual Christians guided by the Spirit. In the terms of this approach the authority of the Bible is established, not primarily through a recognition of the tradition's attestation to it as revelation, but through the strength of its appeal to human reason and its application to ordinary life. We may call this approach "direct reading." Interpretation of the Bible is required, but no institution is needed for this purpose. The essential meaning of scripture and its revelation of God and his purposes are available to every Christian who reads the Bible thoughtfully and prayerfully.

3. In the view of the fundamentalist approach to scripture the Bible needs little or no interpretation. It is not inspired indirectly by God; rather these are his words given directly by the Spirit to the authors of the books of the Bible, and, through the same Spirit, they carry the same meaning in all important ways to people of our own time.

These three basic approaches to the Bible are certainly still in use today, but the first of them, which understands the authority and meaning of the Bible to be mediated through the magisterium of the Church, is not a viable option for most contemporary Christians. Even many Roman Catholics at least question the validity of this way of valuing scripture unless it is understood in the broadest sense which asserts the primacy of community interpretation over that of any individual exegete.[4] For Anglicans and others it is not a live option in any event; there is no official magisterium to do the interpreting.

In the last two centuries there has developed another approach to scripture which has tended for some to replace the interpretative authority of the magisterium: this is historical-critical interpretation. This approach often seems to achieve its authority by claiming to delineate the original circumstances of the biblical writings and the manner in which they were understood during the periods they were being formed and written. The historical-critical approach speaks, it is true, with no single voice. Yet there frequently is a rough kind of consensus, and, in any event, it is an approach which many feel must be heeded if they are to be faithful to the understanding that Christianity is an historical religion. In recent decades this approach has been found to be especially powerful when claiming to give information regarding the message of the historical Jesus as distinct from later community traditions. If one were to try to identify the institutional character of this way of understanding the Bible, one might locate it in the guild of biblical scholars and recognize the ascendancy it has gained through the role these scholars have played in the teaching of future church leaders in our seminaries and universities.

Part I

The historical-critical approach, direct reading, and fundamentalism: these then are three general ways of viewing the Bible
and its authority which I wish to make the major features on my
outline map. I want next to try to show how each of the approaches can result in a mishearing and mishandling of scripture.

A. Historical Criticism

It is not difficult to formulate a glowing public relations
statement to describe what the historical-critical approach is
meant to do. One critic stated its purpose in these terms: ". . . so
to interpret the scriptures that the past becomes alive and illumines
our present with new possibilities for social and personal transformation."[5] I know that I still find much promise in that statement, and I have no doubt that the promise has been partially
fulfilled, at least for some. Yet, after nearly a generation of
teaching in our theological seminaries, and after watching a
series of brilliant colleagues seek "so to interpret the scriptures," I
also have no doubt that the program is not working well at all.

I have seen too many bright and thoughtful seminarians go
forth and evidently fail at the prescribed task. They either
largely abandon the approach from the first (I assume because it
has never really touched their lives), or else they give it up after a
few years (presumably because they were unable to make it bear
fruit in their pastoral and prophetic circumstances). They tell me
they often feel guilty—disloyal to their professors and to an
intellectual tradition. Yet they just cannot make it effective. In
embarrassment they tend either largely to neglect the Bible in
their teaching and preaching[6] or to lapse into an unreflective
crypto-fundamentalism.

For a long time—at least within the theological schools—it
has been felt that there must be something radically wrong in the
culture and in the churches which inhibits the appropriation of
the benefits of the historical-critical method. Or else the trouble
must be with the graduates of these schools. Perhaps they are
not trying hard enough, or they lack the courage to present the

sometimes difficult and sometimes "disenchanting" features of the historical-critical approach to their congregations. Just possibly there may be some flaw in the way the material is taught in the seminaries which appropriate changes in the curriculum might be able to correct. Only in recent years has the awareness grown that there may be serious faults in the approach itself—or at least with the approach when it is presented as though it were virtually the sole way of interpreting scripture with integrity.

There is not sufficient opportunity to speculate on all the reasons for this gap between the promise of historical criticism and its results in the churches, and I am here more concerned with the fact than the causes. We may, however, recognize the tendency of many of those who study the past to be willing to leave it to others to make any attempts to "illumine our present with new possibilities." Indeed, the "guild" of biblical scholars has succeeded so well in protecting itself from many of the questions and the biases of the contemporary churches that oftentimes the most vital of human questions seem to be ruled out of court. In order to define their discipline, and so that it may be seen to be on a par with other "scientific" studies, the methods of scholarship and teaching are frequently restricted to questions dealing only with the past. From this perspective efforts to approach the biblical traditions by beginning with present day concerns and with the passions and polemics of contemporary life can only lead to distortions.

And yet, one has to ask, how well can traditions which themselves were often forged in circumstances of polemic and passion be understood when there is no living analogy? Can dispassionate interpretation ever make us hear the full ranges of the prophet's stern warning or the disciple's song of praise? How well can a predominantly historical interest in the Bible understand writers who were more concerned about the present and future role of their traditions than their past?

Take the role of God in the Bible. In order to perform its task the historical-critical approach, working on the basis of the understanding that all history must be similarly interpreted as a closed system operating on principles of cause and effect, regularly does not raise the question of God's involvement with that history, except perhaps to note its place in the belief of the times. Questions dealing with how and whether God was involved with the lives of biblical figures go either unasked or are set aside, thus also leaving aside issues most central to the traditions.

Decades ago the necessity of the involvement of the exegete in the deep human concerns of his material was forcefully argued by Karl Barth, who then nervously accepted Rudolf Bultmann's vigorous agreement.[7] Yet the historical-critical method, by the very definitions of its approach, has the greatest difficulty in taking such concerns into account. When it is presented to students and others as the only way (or the only significant way) of understanding the Bible, it is hardly any wonder that many contemporary people look elsewhere for their inspiration.

B. Direct Reading

This approach gives highest priority to the common sense of the serious and thoughtful reader of scripture today. It need not wholly dismiss the value of some historical-critical data, although too much of this information might only become confusing. It is human reason, judgment, and experience, with help from the guidance of the Holy Spirit, which enable the Bible to speak clearly and forcefully to contemporary lives. Indeed, one often begins from present day concerns and circumstances and then searches scripture for insight into them.

This way of reading the Bible assumes that there is a form of correspondence between what can be understood by means of natural religious interpretation (through human reason and experience) and the particular revelation of the Bible. This approach, which one can find espoused with different emphases as much in certain ''conservative'' as in ''liberal'' church circles, views the Bible as both a human and a divine document. God acting through human lives guided the events the Bible describes and inspired the authors.[8] Influenced by the same Spirit of God, men and women of today can, through their interpretation, again experience these traditions as living and true. Of course, from time to time uncertainties will arise, but the central teachings remain clear, and, when in doubt, the overall sense of the Bible may be used to interpret any obscure portions. Scripture can then speak directly and simply to our lives. What emerges from this reflection are timeless, religious truths which can often be abstracted from the Bible and applied in all manner of circumstances.

The trouble is that most reflective people do not find the matter all that uncomplicated. The problems surface most obstructively when we notice that different readers and different communities of Christians interpret scripture "simply" in quite variant ways. While we may from time to time wish to rejoice in the "common language" that the biblical stories and traditions provide for all Christians, the fact remains that this language can be, and often is, heard in accents so diverse that mutual understanding is difficult.[9]

What does the Bible tell us about the pros and cons of pacifism or the legitimacy of "just" wars? What do we learn about the rights of ownership in conflict with the demands of the poor? Does the Bible maintain that God has predetermined and controls all events, or is there place for human will acting outside divine direction? What do we learn when we ask for guidance on other specific matters which trouble churches today: Should women be ordained? What should be the response to forms of sexuality outside the marriage covenant?

The frequent counsel to "just go read your Bible" sounds appealing when one is reading the Bible for the pleasure of edification, but what happens when there is controversy? Can just anyone use scripture and act on the authority of their own interpretation of it? I am reminded of a story attributed to Carl Sandburg regarding a group of applicants for a job. Each was given a one question interview: how much is two plus two? All responded four, except for the one who got the job. That person answered, "It amounts to whatever you want it to, sir."

Our approach to the Bible when, for instance, we choose a convenient scripture text for our sermon after we have written it, may not be all that different from the response of Sandburg's successful applicant. Do not most of us have our favorite books and passages from the Bible which we read and those we do not read? Do not liberals and conservatives have their respective

Mary Baker Eddy-like red-lettered versions of the Bible from which they quote the passages they regard as most important? Do not they each tend to sketch their own picture of Jesus by drawing from their favorite sections of the Gospels?[10]

Often by means of this approach we are so little challenged by viewpoints and understandings different from our own that we are not even aware that we are wearing the tinted spectacles of our own culture. One group's legitimate need for perceiving in scripture the model of its own struggle for liberation can, nevertheless, cause it to twist the Exodus story sufficiently out of context and shape as to run the risk of failing to hear some of the challenges the story may have for them.[11] Concerns with our morality may make us deaf to the hearing of stories which seem to fly in the face of our values, like the parable of the unjust steward who, upon learning that he was to be fired, began fiddling with his master's accounts in order to curry favor with his debtors (Luke 16:1-9)—or the story of the vineyard workers who, although all laboring different numbers of hours, were paid the same amount (Matt. 20:1-15).[12] Reading St. Paul's letters while lying on the couch of the psychological preoccupations of western society can easily lead us into such mishearing of his views of human nature and sin that we seriously misappropriate the thrust of his teaching about justification and salvation.[13]

C. Fundamentalism

Since interpretation of scripture apparently involves so much uncertainty and potential misconstruction, it is understandable that a group of Christians has contended that the Bible needs little or no interpretation: There is no place for human judgment to stand before scripture; rather it is human judgment that is being judged.[14] Where other approaches tend to speak of inspiration of the Bible through human beings in some indirect manner, the fundamentalist doctrine of plenary inspiration (which only became firmly articulated in response to the challenge of historical criticism) maintains that each idea and every word of scripture was purposefully and inerrantly inspired by God's Spirit. Moreover, the Bible can be trusted accurately to report the events it describes. Indeed, for most fundamentalists this is the key issue:[15] this errorless record is available to men and women of every time and culture. What it meant and what it means today are, in all important ways, identical. All differences between cultural circumstances and other problems of human understanding are overcome by the transcendent power of the Spirit.

It is easy to caricature fundamentalism, especially in its so-called "hard" version which can be made to defend as actual historical events Joshua's halting of the sun in the sky or Jesus' sending of two thousand pigs into the sea. (Imagine, we say from our non-Hebraic, ecologically-minded perspective, our Lord wasting all that ham and bacon!) There are, however, versions of fundamentalism (so-called "soft" fundamentalism) which acknowledge a measure of surface disagreement and some contribution from a critical as well as historical perspective. There is more concern to maintain that the Bible is so written as in no way to lead disciples into error than to insist on absolute inerrancy. Of course, just because it does permit a degree of interpretative exegesis and a role for human judgment, soft fundamentalism comes in for severe criticism from fundamentalism's more rigoristic defenders.[16]

Still, however it is espoused (or whatever name it may today employ), a fundamentalism which advocates a virtual historical inerrancy of the Bible presents us with serious difficulties. While we can admire and learn from the seriousness with which it confronts scripture, we must also note several of the more significant problems.

The basic fundamentalist position, to put it baldly, does not correspond with the information and insights which thinking people gain from a thoughtful reading of scripture and from historical study. Given all the difficulties of trying to ascertain what can be "known" historically, that may sound like an unsophisticated statement. One can respond that the evaluation of historical material is regularly influenced by attitudes which have little to do with historical data. Thus one's approach to scripture need not be dictated to by currently prevailing perspectives on history.

Yet I cannot agree that we are being faithful to the evidence we have if we suggest that an appropriate approach to the Bible may be regarded as more a matter of opinion than of truth. Contrary to the a-intellectualism of much of our society, not everything is ultimately a matter of taste and attitude. Whether or not we might wish it otherwise, and that we had an inerrant, infallible book factually reporting things as they happened and were said at the time, it is clear that the various books of the Bible have emerged from the crucible of tensions and paradoxes of human history. In the process of its composition it has been written and rewritten, interpreted and reinterpreted in circumstances which have not escaped fallibility and ambiguity. However else we may come to maintain that scripture is inspired, God has worked through history and human lives in ways other than an uncritical fundamentalism allows. We have no choice but to try to interpret scripture. The question is how we are to do this.

Efforts to mask the fact that all of us must interpret scripture and that we tend to read the Bible selectively can leave us quite unaware of our prejudices. Fundamentalists may concentrate on, for example, passages having to do with sexuality while ignoring (or suddenly becoming highly interpretative) when it comes to words such as these: "Lord, who may enter your Temple? Who may worship on Zion your sacred hill? . . . He (who) makes loans without charging interest . . . . (Psalm 15:1, 5. Today's English Version).

Because fundamentalism acknowledges no critical cultural gap between our age and biblical times, one may all too readily employ the Bible as a bulwark for unexamined national and cultural prejudices. There is little challenge to view the human condition and history from perspectives other than our own. With this comes the danger of asking the Bible for answers to questions which were never posed when it was being written—or, at the least, which would never have been posed in our terms. Our century's preoccupation with whether things "happened" in exactly the way described and the insistence that meaning and value depend on this factor alone is one example. (This concern has sometimes made the fundamentalists and the critical historians into an oddly mated couple in the debate—both of them often seeming to insist that the only real value of scripture is to be found in its use as a record of past events.)

One need scarcely mention what an uncritical preoccupation with matching narrative and descriptive language to historical event does to the character of the creation story or the poetry of apocalypse. In the arena of ethics the danger of insisting upon surface understanding and legalistic application without probing for deeper meaning is still more pronounced. Jesus said, "If anyone strike you on the right cheek, turn to him the other also" (Matt. 5:39). Is it Christian to stand there and let another person (perhaps a madman) beat one to a pulp?

Finally, in this regard, there is a tendency for fundamentalism, by flattening out the hills and valleys of paradox and tension in the Bible, to give us answers where the Bible may actually be inviting us toward greater adventures. The power of many different uses of language—of myth, symbol, metaphor, humor, and irony—to draw us beyond the boundaries we set for ourselves is too often muffled by trivial concerns with historical and verbal accuracy. Is the Bible meant to tell us what life is all about or to lure us toward the frontier of the kingdom and the mystery of new possibilities for life in relationship with God? In the last analysis is it in the Bible that we find ultimate truth or is the Bible not meant to witness beyond itself to the truth that is Christ?

Part II

How may we read and hear our Bibles faithfully? So far I have rather pushed us into a corner by suggesting that the major approaches to scripture used today are seriously flawed. Indeed, they have been used in such ways as to make the Bible seem ineffective and insipid in our lives. In order to make my points, to make the features on our sketch map stand out more clearly, I have admittedly indulged in some over-simplification and caricature. I now, however, wish to try to make amends and to maintain that these same three approaches, when properly employed in a dynamic interrelationship with one another, and so understood rather differently, can open for us the broad avenue that is needed if the authoritative power and the passion of the Bible is to stream into our lives.[17]

A. Historical Criticism

The perspective and insights offered by this approach are indispensable for the Christian community, especially for those who are the stewards and teachers of the foundational traditions of the faith.[18] The disciplines of historical criticism[19] can help us to hear and to feel the pulse and color of living people—individuals and communities—who struggled to give expression to their awareness of God moving within the events of history and human lives. The stories and sayings, the prophecy and poetry, again take on the dimensions and tones of real people with whom we can imagine relationship and through whom we may recognize the activity of both the courses of history and the power of the Holy Spirit.

Yet, despite our frequent protestations with regard to the significance of the historical character of the Christian religion, we cannot help but be aware that there is within many of us a resistance to viewing scripture as a compilation of quite diverse traditions emerging from the actual vicissitudes of history. A part of us wants a form of inspiration less subject to human frailties and ambiguities. When we confront the tougher issues of faith (having to do with dearly held ideas about early church practice or, for example, our understanding of the resurrection and Jesus' divinity), we often pass over the scriptures lightly (making use, perhaps, of a "proof" text here or there) and resort to a brand of creedal literalism. Sometimes our most heartfelt question to the biblical exegetes seems to be "How can I use the Bible so it won't destroy my faith?"

In our better moments, however, we recognize that the very toughness of these issues can provide us with the solid food which is necessary for our growth and maturity as Christians. This is the nourishment which can wean us away from childish attitudes and ways of enacting our Christianity which may never lead us toward "the measure of the stature of the fulness of Christ" (Eph. 4:13). We who live amid the ups and downs and uncertainties of historical change need and want a faith which was born and grew in circumstances at least analogous to our own. History is the inescapable context for our faith.

At the theological school where I teach, one of the first programs that students confront is an intensive introduction to Greek. Complaints are not infrequent from students and sometimes their sponsors. Is this really necessary when there are so many other pressing needs and opportunities for ministry? My smart-aleck but still seriously intentioned response is that we intend to leave all our students with the indelible impression that the New Testament was written in a language other than their own. In the heat of discussions about the meaning of various passages of scripture it is all too easy to forget that each language functions differently from others and that there can never be a direct translation from, for example, a Greek word or phrase to a similar expression in English. Arguments based on Paul's interpretation of "justification" or "being made right" "by faith" easily go awry when they fail to recognize how hard it is to render Paul's idea into English.

Beginning with this awareness we can go on to recognize how misleading it may be to assume that a scriptural image readily conveys to us the same range of meanings it offered in its earlier contexts. Our own concerns, for example, with matters of paternalism and sexism might cause us to misconstrue or fail to hear the various nuances of "fatherhood" imbedded in the Bible.[20] Similarly, we had best not try to make use of sayings about divorce in the New Testament without recognizing that most women of the time had no legal standing and desperately needed some form of protection.

From among the many passages one might choose to illustrate the values of the historical-critical approach let us look briefly at the parable of the sower (Mark 4:3-20)—the story of the man who sowed seed on a path, on hard ground, among thorns and on good soil, with very different results. First of all, historical insights help us to recognize that an understanding of the story depends on a way of planting different from the practice with which we are familiar. Redaction criticism helps us to see how fully Mark has made the parable part of his Gospel by making use of an allegorical interpretation which explains the difficulties encountered by the missionary activity of the community. Matthew and Luke have given the story their own emphases. Behind these versions, however, one might glimpse an earlier unallegorized parable concerned with the mysterious and surprising character of the kingdom's advent.[21] After New Testament times, on the other hand, there is a long and honorable homiletic tradition which has used the story to reflect on the dangers and opportunities for individual Christian discipleship.

On occasion there has been an unfortunate tendency among biblical critics to suggest that one version and interpretation of such a story may be right and others wrong, the right one usually being regarded as the earliest presentation. A more proper use of historical criticism recognizes that there need be no one meaning, much less one correct meaning for a story. Some of the understandings sketched above may have more value for us than others. We may be especially interested in how the story seems to have been understood in the context of a particular Gospel when that Gospel was first being used.[22] But all these understandings can play their role in helping us to appreciate the full range of insights made available by the parable of the sower and the variety of ways through which the Holy Spirit may have acted in the rehearing of the narrative.

Similarly we should beware of the tendency to harmonize and to try to gloss over or to resolve the tensions between different passages and books of the Bible. In the past we have been offered the analogy of the many voices comprising one choir as a way to harmonize the apparent dissonances. "There are those who feel, on the contrary," James Barr suggests, "that the diversity and disagreement found within the Bible is a more sure characteristic of its nature and a more promising clue to its meaning."[23] In these terms we would maintain, for example, that the often quite different ways of talking about the significance of Jesus found in the New Testament can help draw us toward a far more profound awareness of who he has been and who he can be in our lives.

Viewed along these lines we might understand the historical-critical approach as providing us with a kind of modern-day magisterium for our interpretation of scripture—not necessarily offering us one definitive meaning for a particular passage, but frequently helping us to recognize a range of insights (of ways of probing the deep mysteries of faith) from a long, living community of discipleship. So may we gain a keener appreciation of the handing on of tradition, and of how and why it is that these materials have been told and retold in many contexts and have served as the models or master stories of the church, continuously shaping the life of the community and the nature of faith.[24]

B. Direct Reading

Such historical-critical analysis of how scripture was once understood cannot by itself make the Bible heard in our lives. There must be some form of new incarnation of the story or other biblical passage within our living circumstances—some opportunity for the story to speak directly to us and for ourselves to "live" in the story—before new insight can be ours. This direct reading or direct appropriation of a biblical story, I want now to suggest, can in fact happen in a great variety of ways.

Several years ago, when my children were younger and the family took long car trips at vacation time, I found it convenient to read the daily offices as we were traveling. Since the children liked to read aloud and it was a way of involving them I would ask them to read the Old and New Testament lessons. Later we discussed them. Many of the lessons, of course, lent themselves to relatively edifying conversations. When it came to some of the more gruesome parts of the Bible, I was, however, chagrined and even horrified by the nature of their enthusiastic interest. They were vastly intrigued by the slaughter of the Amalekites and the final hacking into pieces of poor King Agag. With respect to the crucifixion of our Lord and Savior Jesus Christ their questions ran along these lines: Did it hurt a lot? How much did he bleed? How long did it take him to die? One day not long after I caught them out in the backyard crucifying their G.I. Joe doll.

I spent some time trying to divert their interests into more wholesome paths or at the least to offer more instructive understandings of these events. Finally it dawned on me, however,

38   SCRIPTURE TODAY

that there might well be times when the stories did not need all my efforts at interpretation. In fact, in due course the stories did prompt in my sons a number of theological and historical questions which will arise pretty much of themselves in people being educated in this last part of the twentieth century. But first the boys had heard the story—a point, I would add, of critical importance for all Christian education.[25] I am convinced that one of the mistakes often made in teaching the Bible today is that we tend to give students the "results" of historical-critical study before they have ever really been asked to read the Bible for themselves and so let many of the questions which historical criticism is trying to deal with first become their own questions.

Now it is true that some of the biblical narratives (e.g., Jesus' resurrection) will raise more acute questions about historical accuracy than do others whose authority is far less explicitly related to historical events (e.g., Job, Jesus' parables). Nor are all scriptural materials found in story form, although all can be heard within the frame of larger stories about the community or discipleship. Many of the passages do, however, have the power to speak directly to us—to excite our own thoughts and emotions and to awaken in us our own deep concerns about the existence of God, the role of evil and suffering, the grounds for hope and enduring values.

In order for this to happen, however, we must sometimes cultivate what has been called a "second naiveté,"[26] a capacity, not to dismiss our historical critical faculties (indeed, they can well be employed to help us gain access to the past uses of a story), but to allow for a time other interests to play their roles. Interpretation can help the story or myth, the song or prophecy, to speak to us on its own terms. We then become aware that "direct reading" may actually involve many different levels of hearing which can communicate forcefully to us. Hearing in this way, we no longer make the mistake of asking "what one meaning does this passage of the Bible have that we can take away from it," but rather "what are the various insights which we may realize as we share in the narrative character or setting of the passage?" The story of the raising of Lazarus (John 11:1-53) offers one case in point with its deep ironies and probings of

how life might overcome death. Or consider the story of Zac-
chaeus (Luke 19:1-10)—a triumph of the healing power of
acceptance over the disease and loneliness of greed. Or we might
think of Legion and the casting out, and tricking into their
destruction, of the demons which bind men to a living death
(Mark 5:1-20).

Each story, we may recognize, has its historical and diachronic
dimensions. It is a story fashioned in some relation to historical
circumstances and with its own history of retelling and interpretation. Each story may, however, also be viewed as timeless. It
has its particular structural features and synchronic dimensions
which, beyond the many changes that take place in societies, can
be heard speaking to deeper aspects of all human understanding
and existence.[27] The Bible presents us with the opportunity to
hear its stories in the context of a dialectic, in a context in which
we too stand inside the movement of history while hearing,
perceiving, and imagining in ways that transcend time's flow.

The story-form was so important to Israel and to the first
communities of Christians not because they had some desire to
record a perfectly accurate account of events. That, of course,
cannot be done in any case. What the form allowed them to do
was to contour what had happened so as to begin to bring out,
for themselves and others, the significance of their experience
and what they had been told about the past. This narrative
shaping is both "history-like"[28] (related to historical events and
the historical character of all life) while yet seeking to point, in
and through the story, to the possibility of some design for life.
And here we tread on the frontier of profoundest mystery—the
possibility that we give story-form to what happens to us in life
because God himself (the God who encourages us by most
revealing himself in our stories of exodus, exile and return,
crucifixion and resurrection) is so shaping all life and all understanding so as to include us in his story. The Bible's stories, we
come to realize, are not just illustrations of what can be more
clearly expressed in other ways. Rather, it is through such narratives that the gospel happens.

From the perspective of this frontier we recognize how the
stories and other biblical materials can speak directly to us while

sounding in many different keys. The myths, parables, psalms, and visions—and the metaphors and symbols which live in and arise out of them—are at once simple and profound, but never simplistic. Many of them can engage the child, while at the same time drawing us beyond understanding and to the far limit of imagination. Our greatest abuse of the Bible would be a failure to hear scripture on as many levels of our being as are open to us. It is certainly one of the church's critical evangelical tasks to find—through word-of-mouth, drama, liturgy, song, and painting—a great variety of ways and contexts to retell its master stories. And the retelling is so crucial! It takes living voices of faith and conviction to make the scriptures a living tradition.

The stories are then meant to act as catalysts, encouraging us to live out enacted parables and helping us to interpret what happens to us and to tell new stories of the divine possibility in the midst of our lives. These experiences, in their turn, then make us better able to appreciate the biblical narratives. This is an aspect of what one critic has spoken of as "a hermeneutic of engagement."[29] In order to be more fully understood, scriptural passages must be heard, interpreted, and acted upon—not just by individuals, but again within the context of a contemporary community of believers who are themselves struggling and endeavoring to live faithfully with questions and issues at least analogous to those which preoccupied the patriarchs and prophets of Israel and the disciples of Jesus. Not only is it unavoidable that interpreters must become part of the interpretative process, there are many occasions in which that involvement must be eagerly sought if scripture is again to become a living Word, and, indeed, if one is to have any genuine sense of how and why these issues mattered in their own time.[30]

C. Fundamentalism

Finally I wish to maintain that it is the multivocal hearing of scripture within our own personal and community settings of faith involvement (our direct reading), done in critical relation to the understandings of those who first experienced and interpreted biblical events, which can provide the context for a profound, *fundamental* engagement with the Bible. I want to own that word and to claim to be a fundamental interpreter of scripture.[31] I wish to claim this to be true for all those who take scripture seriously and who have come to discover (not just on the authority of an institution or previous testimony but in their own personal and communal lives) that in the hearing of the Bible they may realize a transcendent mystery acting immanently through human experience and reflection on that experience. It is this awareness of God's presence through scripture which causes them to return to the Bible again and again in the faith that revelation does and will happen. It is this expectation and the belief that the Bible points beyond itself to God that makes genuine fundamentalists—deep probers of the fundamental significance of scripture. What the Bible then offers is not so much solutions to life's problems as help in discovering the direction in which to face if answers are to be found.

This penetrating hearing of scripture presents a far more awesome challenge than a concern with establishing some one meaning of scripture which can often become frozen at a surface level of comprehension. Let us recall those words about turning the cheek: "If anyone strikes you on the right cheek, turn to him the other also." (Matt. 5:39). Indeed, there may be times when one can and should fulfill that command to the letter, but genuine fundamentalism points to our Lord's far more pervasive demand that his disciples must never act in revenge.

What are we to do with our gospel stories which speak of demons and their exorcism? Frequently we seem to be given a Hobson's choice. We are, on the one hand, to attempt the feat of importing an acceptance of the actuality of demons (as we imagine first century people conceived of them) straight into the century of television and computer technology. If we cannot achieve this feat, then our only other choice seems to be to relegate the language about demons to a primitive mythology from a superstitious culture which we are right to ignore from the pulpit and in counseling and spiritual direction.

Genuine fundamentalism, however, works at a deeper level. It probes what it was that first century Christians were trying to express. It engages our experience of forces which are part of our

own psyches but which also are our enemies and at times threaten
to overwhelm us. Guilt, covert anger, anxiety, fear, and loneliness
can make us sick spiritually and emotionally, and sometimes
physically as well. Then, too, we recognize powers abroad in
society which are partly of our own making yet greater than the
sum of their parts. We seem compelled into compliance by the
spirits of militarism, sexism, racism, and the insatiable insecurities
which, through the demand for not only enough but an unlimited
more than enough, foster the gross economic injustices and
environmental disasters of our planet. There is a great and
terrible madness loose in the world, and we, too, long for a power
greater than our own which can liberate us and enable us to
overcome these demonic forces.[32]

One further example. That parable of the steward who, upon
learning that he is soon to be fired, resorts to juggling his master's
accounts in order to curry future favor with his debtors (Luke
16:1-9) is regularly not commented upon in church school or
from the pulpit. Its surface message offends our understanding
of common morality. The evangelist has given us some assistance
by interpreting the story as a lesson in the shrewdness with which
disciples are to deal with the world. More recent interpreters
have helped us to see that the narrative can be heard as a comic
parable inciting disciples to face up to the facts of life, just as
realistically as this steward, when the challenge and judgment of
the kingdom approaches. Calamity may be seized upon as new
opportunity. Perhaps still more fundamentally we are invited to
participate in the story as individuals and as a community who
are always in danger of being found to be inadequate or dishonest.
What will we do if we then are also too ashamed to beg and too
old to dig ditches? Or, transposed into other terms, when circumstances seem to overwhelm us, when evil mounts up, when
crucifixion seems the end of all hope; will we find the mysterious
power to go on trying anyway, even like this rascally steward?
At its heart the parable suddenly becomes for us a story about
death and the possibility of new life.[33]

There is a sense in which every biblical passage shares in, and
is informed by, the great master story of Jesus' passion, moving
through the dark horror of crucifixion to the Easter dawn. The

words of the Bible which tell these stories are never ends in themselves but are always pointing beyond themselves to the one who is known to us through his story. And always these words come to us, not just as a message of hope and not just as judgment, but always as challenge and grace in the same moment. In this way many of the sayings and parables of Jesus seem especially designed to force open cracks in our surface readings of the meaning of life. We are left standing on unsettling ground.[34] There we are made to glimpse fundamental depths where the nature and purpose of our lives and our community are brought radically into question, but where we may also catch sight of the foundation of all hope.

Notes

1. Cf. also II Tim. 3:15-17. Both the context and phrasing of Rom. 15:4 may indicate that there was already some questioning of the status of the authority of Jewish scriptures for Gentile Christians and also the beginning of a concern with regard to precisely which writings were to be regarded as of God. For introductory surveys of the issues see the articles "Canon of the OT" (D. N. Freedman), "Canon of the NT" (A. C. Sundberg, Jr.), "Biblical Theology" (J. Barr), and "Scripture, Authority of" (J. Barr) in the Supplementary Volume to *The Interpreter's Dictionary of the Bible,* ed. K. Crim (Nashville: Abingdon, 1976). The series of articles "Interpretation, History of" in the same volume can be supplemented by the three volumes of *The Cambridge History of the Bible* (Cambridge University Press); I. *From the Beginnings to Jerome* (ed. P. R. Ackroyd and C. F. Evans, 1970); II. *The West from the Fathers to the Reformation* (ed. G. W. H. Lampe, 1969); III. *The West from the Reformation to the Present Day* (ed. G. L. Greenslade, 1963). Many of the issues touched upon in this essay are discussed by James Barr in *The Bible in the Modern World* (New York, etc: Harper, 1973). For an introduction to the manner in which many of the issues have developed, cf. W. G. Kümmel, *The New Testament: The History of the Investigation of its Problems,* tr. S. M. Gilmour and H. C. Kee (Nashville: Abingdon, 1972). A good basic presentation, with sympathy for the more conservative approaches, is provided by David Stacey's *Interpreting the Bible* (New York: Hawthorn Books, 1977).

2. This awareness is given special stress by Dennis Nineham in *The Use and Abuse of the Bible: A Study of the Bible in an Age of Rapid*

Cultural Change (New York, etc: Harper, 1976). Nineham emphasizes the ways in which the gap between world views has become particularly pronounced in the last several centuries. See p. 55.

3. This point is particularly well made by André Benoit, ''The Transmission of the Gospel in the First Centuries'' in *The Gospel as History,* ed. V. Vajta (Philadelphia: Fortress, 1975) pp. 145-168, especially as he stresses the awareness that all transmission of tradition involves interpretation.

4. For a good discussion of questions of biblical authority and ways of viewing inspiration by a Roman Catholic biblical scholar, see Bruce Vawter's *Biblical Inspiration* (Philadelphia: Westminster, 1972).

5. So Walter Wink, himself a sharp critic of the historical-critical method as it is often used, in *The Bible in Human Transformation: toward a new paradigm for biblical study* (Philadelphia: Fortress, 1973) p. 2.

6. For an analysis of this neglect (which would apply only to the so-called liberal churches), see J. D. Smart, *The Strange Silence of the Bible in the Church: a Study in Hermeneutics* (Philadelphia: Westminster, 1970). Note his critique of seminary teaching of the Bible and his suggestions to help give the Bible contemporary relevance, pp. 151-172. A still more spirited defense of the historical-critical approach to the Bible and its importance for making the Bible a living force in individual lives and in the churches is his *The Past, Present and Future of Biblical Theology* (Philadelphia: Westminster, 1979).

7. See the prefaces to the second and then the third editions of Barth's *The Epistle to the Romans.* For a more contemporary German critique of the historical-critical approach when used autonomously, see Peter Stuhlmacher, *Historical Criticism and Theological Interpretation of Scriptures: Toward a Hermeneutics of Consent,* tr. Roy A. Harrisville (Philadelphia: Fortress, 1977). From Barth's perspective Krister Stendahl's often referred to distinction between ''what [a biblical writing] meant'' in its own time and ''what it means'' today (see ''Biblical Theology, Contemporary'' *The Interpreter's Dictionary of the Bible,* Vol. I, pp. 418-432) would lead to certain misinterpretation if the processes were kept wholly separate. Then see Stendahl's sharp critique of Barth, *op. cit.,* p. 420.

8. In an effort to locate more definitively just where and how revelation takes place, some scholars have tended to regard revelation as being in the events of the Bible themselves which are then witnessed to by fallible human beings. Others, however, understand God's activity to be

more in the lives of the witnesses than in the events they are interpreting. Both views present complex problems (cf. Barr, *The Bible in the Modern World,* especially pp. 75-88) and neither seems able to stand by itself.

9. Cf. the study report "The Authority of the Bible" in *The Ecumenical Review,* 21 (1969) pp. 135-166.

10. The dangers have nowhere been better stated than by H. J. Cadbury in *The Peril of Modernizing Jesus* (New York: Macmillan, 1937).

11. Compare, for instance, John Howard Yoder's reading of the Exodus narrative from a pacifist perspective in *The Politics of Jesus: Vicit Agnus Noster* (Grand Rapids, Mich: Eerdmans, 1972) pp. 79-82.

12. On the parable of the unjust steward see also below p. 27, and on the interpretation of both these stories, cf. F. H. Borsch, *God's Parable* (Philadelphia: Westminster, 1976) pp. 55-67.

13. See Krister Stendahl's significant and provocative essay "The Apostle Paul and the Introspective Conscience of the West," *Harvard Theological Review,* 56 (1963) pp. 199-215, reprinted with related materials in his *Paul Among Jews and Gentiles and Other Essays* (Philadelphia: Fortress, 1976) pp. 78-96.

14. Cf., for example, "The Chicago Statement on Biblical Inerrancy," *Journal of the Evangelical Theological Society,* 21 (1978) pp. 289-296.

Fundamentalism is a term of comparatively recent vintage (apparently taken from a series of pamphlets entitled *The Fundamentals*) which came into use in the early part of this century to describe certain groups of Christians in the United States who rigidly upheld what were regarded as traditional orthodox Christian doctrines, among them the inerrancy of scripture. It is now often used more broadly to refer to this general position with respect to scripture.

15. On this point see James Barr, *Fundamentalism* (Philadelphia: Westminster, 1976), especially pp. 40-55, and more generally for a comprehensive and penetrating critique of fundamentalist theology and biblical interpretation.

16. So Harold Lindsell, *The Battle for the Bible* (Grand Rapids, Mich.: Zondervan, 1976). Contrast the searching and sometimes agonized exploration by Robert K. Johnston, *Evangelicals at an Impasse: Biblical Authority in Practice* (Richmond, Va.: John Knox, 1979) especially pp. 1-47. A balanced viewpoint from a conservative but not fundamentalist biblical scholar is presented by G. E. Ladd's *The New Testament and Criticism* (Grand Rapids, Mich.: Eerdmans, 1967).

17. In the context of the Trinity Institute Conference it seems apt to note that these three approaches can be seen to correspond with the

time-honored Anglican addresses to scripture—scripture read and heard in the light of the Christian community's tradition and experienced reason while valued as revelation. Cf., e.g., F. D. Maurice's discussion in *The Kingdom of Christ or Hints to a Quaker Respecting the Principles, Constitution and Order of the Catholic Church* (New York: Macmillan, 4th ed., 1891) Vol. II, pp. 178 ff.

18. Recently James Barr has asked the question whether the historical-critical reading of the Bible should best be regarded as a secular instrument, perhaps of some use to theology, or whether it draws legitimation from within the structure of Christian belief and, therefore, of valid theological thinking. See his paper "Historical Reading and the Historical Interpretation of Scripture" to be published in the *Journal of Theological Studies.* In answering the question in favor of the latter understanding Barr makes the point that the reading must not only be historical (as in some fundamentalist approaches) but critical. Cf. also his discussion of the ranges of meaning of these terms.

19. It is important to recognize that historical criticism is far more of an art form than one specific 'scientific' discipline. It makes use of a series of disciplines involving different kinds of argument. See V. A. Harvey's discussion of history as a "field-encompassing field" in *The Historian and the Believer: The Morality of Historical Knowledge and Christian Belief* (New York: Macmillan, 1966) pp. 49-67. Cf. also J. D. Crossan, "Perspectives and Methods in Contemporary Biblical Criticism," *Biblical Research,* 22 (1977) pp. 39-49.

20. See Robert Hamerton-Kelly, *God the Father: Theology and Patriarchy in the Teaching of Jesus* (Philadelphia: Fortress, 1979), who understands the father symbolism in the Bible to be essentially concerned with liberation and human maturity.

21. Further on this way of viewing the parable, see my *God's Parable,* pp. 51-52. Now cf. also J. D. Crossan, *Cliffs of Fall: Paradox and Polyvalence in the Parables of Jesus* (New York: Seabury, 1980).

22. Brevard S. Childs has led the recent thrust in biblical criticism which holds up the finished and fully composed writings of the Old and New Testaments at the time they have become published and recognized as authoritative ("canonical") for the community as the decisive stages on which historical interpretation should concentrate. See his *Introduction to the Old Testament as Scripture* (Philadelphia: Fortress, 1979), especially pp. 27-106. "The significance of the final form of the biblical text is that it alone bears witness to the full history of revelation." pp. 75-76. Childs has vital points to make. I would, however, also want to

single out the 'moment' when individual New Testament writings began to be valued as authoritative as of critical importance, and continue to maintain that a comprehensive biblical criticism, involving research of the pre-history of the text as well as its final form and later use, need not result in irresolvable conflict and is valuable for a full appreciation of the inspiration of scripture.

23. J. Barr, *The Bible in the Modern World,* p. 6.

24. On the ways in which foundational stories fashion and foster community see F. H. Borsch, *Introducing the Lessons of the Church Year: A Guide for Lay Readers and Congregations* (New York: Seabury, 1978) pp. 4-7.

25. See the commentary on this point and the setting forth of an approach to help achieve a multileveled hearing of the Bible in the churches by Joseph P. Russell, *Sharing our Biblical Story: A Guide to Using Liturgical Readings as the Core of Church and Family Education* (Minneapolis: Winston, 1979).

26. So Paul Ricoeur, *The Symbolism of Evil,* tr. E. Buchanan (Boston: Beacon, 1969) pp. 351-352. ". . . we can, we modern men, aim at a second naiveté in and through criticism. In short, it is by *interpreting* that we can *hear* again." Ricoeur advocates this manner of approach to mythical materials, but it could well be used with respect to many types of narrative including those based on historical incident.

27. See the discussions by W. A. Beardslee in *Literary Criticism of the New Testament* (Philadelphia: Fortress, 1970), especially pp. 1-29; E. V. McKnight, *Meaning in Texts: the Historical Shaping of a Narrative Hermeneutics* (Philadelphia: Fortress, 1978); and, focusing much more specifically and technically on structuralism, *What is Structural Exegesis?* by Daniel Patte (Philadelphia: Fortress, 1976). A helpful statement regarding the way that historical-diachronic and literary-structural, along with other synchronic approaches, can work together was made by Norman Perrin in *Jesus and the Language of the Kingdom: Symbol and Metaphor in New Testament Interpretation* (Philadelphia: Fortress, 1976). *Semeia: an experimental journal for biblical criticism* (distributed by Scholar's Press, Missoula, MT) concentrates its interest on issues of structure, style and literary analysis. Further on the story form and scripture, cf. Steven Crites, "The Narrative Quality of Experience" in *The Journal of the American Academy of Religion,* 39 (1971) pp. 291-311; Sallie M. TeSelle, *Speaking in Parables: a Study in Metaphor and Theology* (Philadelphia: Fortress, 1975); and J. B. Wiggins, ed., *Religion as Story* (New York: Harper, 1975). See also the useful discussion by

Stanley Hauerwas in his chapter "Story and Theology" in *Truthfulness and Tragedy: Further Investigations into Christian Ethics* (Notre Dame, Ind.: University of Notre Dame, 1977) pp. 71-81. One should particularly note his salutary concern with the possible misuses of the story approach to theology.

28. Cf. the use and discussion of this phrase (based in part on the work of Erich Auerbach in *Mimesis: the Representation of Reality in Western Literature,* tr. Willard Trask [Princeton: Princeton University, 1953]) by Hans Frei in *The Eclipse of Biblical Narrative: a Study in Eighteenth and Nineteenth Century Hermeneutics* (New Haven: Yale University, 1974), especially in his "Introduction," pp. 1-16. Frei goes on to show how the development of historical criticism and other intellectual movements during the eighteenth and nineteenth centuries have resulted in a profound change in the ways in which biblical narratives are read. The stress on questions of historical accuracy and the concern with the 'meaning' of passages have often caused the realistic and history-like character of biblical narratives to go unattended and unappreciated. See the helpful discussion proposing ways to make use of Frei's and Ricoeur's insights by O. C. Edwards, Jr. in "Historical-Critical Method's Failure of Nerve and a Prescription for a Tonic: a Review of Some Recent Literature" in *Anglican Theological Review,* 59 (1977) pp. 115-134.

29. See P. D. Hanson, *Dynamic Transcendence: the Correlation of Confessional Heritage and Contemporary Experience in a Biblical Model of Divine Activity* (Philadelphia: Fortress, 1978). Not dissimilar approaches are advocated by other critics; e.g., Peter Stuhlmacher, who speaks of a "hermeneutics of consent" and "openness to transcendence" in *Historical Criticism and Theological Interpretation of Scripture.* It is certainly of interest in this regard that D. H. Kelsey finds that most theologians' use of scripture is seminally influenced by their a priori understanding of God's mode of presence in the world which, in turn, is largely formed by the understanding imparted to them by their churches. It is in this context that the Bible is then used authoritatively in theology. Bible texts taken as scriptures may be said to assume an authority for a Christian community when "they provide patterns determinate enough to *function* as the basis for assessment of the Christian aptness of current churchly forms of life and speech and of theologians' proposals for reform of that life and speech." *The Uses of Scripture in Recent Theology* (Philadelphia: Fortress, 1975) p. 194.

30. With respect to the role of the interpreter in engagement with the text, and with particular reference to the views of Ernst Fuchs, Gerhard

Ebeling and H. G. Gadamer, see the essay "The New Hermeneutic" by A. C. Thiselton in *New Testament Interpretation: Essays on Principles and Methods,* ed. I. H. Marshall (Exeter: Paternoster, 1977) pp. 308-333. This series of essays by generally conservative biblical scholars could serve as a very helpful further introduction to many of the issues here under discussion. It also contains a useful bibliography.

31. Although he has more radical points to make, see the discussion by J. D. Crossan regarding "Jesus' Parable as Fundamental Morality" and "Fundamental Morality and Practical Morality" in *Finding is the First Act: Trove Folktales and Jesus' Treasure Parable* (Philadelphia: Fortress and Missoula, MT: Scholars, 1979) pp. 110-117.

32. Some of the most powerful examples of "fundamental" biblical interpretation in the terms in which we are speaking have emerged from the work of liberation theologians. E.g., Jose Miranda, *Being and the Messiah: the Message of St. John,* tr. John Eagleson (Maryknoll, NY: Orbis, 1977).

33. See again my *God's Parable,* pp. 55-58.

34. Paul Ricoeur ("Biblical Hermeneutics" in *Semeia,* 4 [1975] p. 71) speaks of the process of *reorientation* by *disorientation* as one of the strategies of biblical language. Ricoeur's insight is quoted by W. A. Beardslee in his article "Saving One's Life and Losing It" in the *Journal of the American Academy of Religion,* 47 (1979) pp. 57-72, which is one of a series of contributions in this number subtitled "Thematic Issue: New Testament Interpretation from a Process Perspective." Beardslee believes that the process perspective of interpretation offers an approach which can helpfully relate a rhetorical or phenomenological-literary analysis of biblical materials with the historical-literary point of view. Further on these ways of analysis see Robert Detweiler's *Story, Sign, and Self: Phenomenology and Structuralism as Literary-Critical Methods* (Philadelphia: Fortress and Missoula, MT: Scholars, 1978).

Pastoral Hermeneutics

*Peggy A. Way**

I have chosen the "modest" task of redefining with you, not for you, the entire discipline of pastoral care, pastoral counseling, and pastoral theology. In doing so, I am inviting you to be what in fact you are: that is, a holy people in ecclesial places, creating a hermeneutical style of interpreting existence, without embarrassment and with a strong sense of pride and special calling in who we are and who we are about to be. Our approach to the task is comprised of four elements: salutation, foundation, interpretation, and implication.

I. Salutation

The salutation is not accidental. Many times the salutation is just a greeting. The salutation of my presentation is intrinsic to the whole process and content of my presentation. I am choosing to address you as holy people in ecclesial places, who respond to a spirit of Christian community that you value as a paradigm of human existence. There was an alternative form of address that I had thought to use. I was tempted to begin saying, "Dear brothers and sisters in Christ Jesus, I address you as managers, bureaucrats, spiritual directors, resourcers, counselors, consultants,

Peggy Way is Assistant Professor of Pastoral Theology and Counseling at the Divinity School at Vanderbilt University. She is an expert in the field of pastoral hermeneutics—the subject of her article—and keenly interested in the ways in which scriptural interpretation informs diverse aspects of day-to-day pastoral ministry.

conflict managers, shamans, goal setters, educators, group leaders, administrators, personnel experts, evaluators, politicians, priests, budget builders, small church builders, large church organizers, committee leaders, vulnerable wounded healers, scholars, saints, learned ministers, shepherds, holy ones, and credible bearers of good news.'' That would speak to your fragmentation.

But I want to address you at the center of your being: holy people, called by God to live in the midst of Christian community and who are about the theological task of existence clarification in terms of the Scriptural background and our whole theological tradition. There are other ways of address that I could have chosen but did not: as pastoral counselors, out of some specific therapeutic point of view; or as what Howard Clinebell in his latest book on growth counseling thinks you ought to be—growth coaches—although I do not think we should be growth coaches; or as Jungian interpreters of male/female existence, although I do not think we are primarily Jungian therapists either; or, as what, in terms of the latest new technical discovery, might in the South be called biblical therapists. I could have chosen any of these forms of address, but in each case I would have been addressing you in terms of a specialization that many times has been mistaken for pastoral care or pastoral counseling.

Thus it is crucial that I address you at this certain center in order to deal with the topic of "Scripture Today: Handling the Word Rightly." The perspective out of which I am approaching the task of pastoral hermeneutics is that of pastoral care, pastoral theology, pastoral counseling. That is my academic discipline. What I am saying to you as priests-pastors in the midst of Christian community is that my discipline cannot be properly understood—and the role of Scripture and the Word can not be rightly utilized in it—unless we shift our self-understanding of the pastor and priest, and unless we basically redefine the discipline from that identified by psychology to that identified by Scripture, tradition, and us as holy people in ecclesial places.

This shift that I am making, I am starting to refer to as "pastoral hermeneutics," which simply means pastoral interpretation. This involves our theological tasks of living with our people—in our caring and our counseling—so that what is disclosed on the margins of our contact with them is the meaning of life. It also involves recognizing the way in which the Scriptural tradition informs that meaning, so that we have words to offer our people when they come. I am formally defining pastoral hermeneutics as the interpretation of historical existence in ecclesial context—in the Church—in which we attend to the religious and theological dimensions of human existence as they show up at the intersections of our ministries with particular persons.

Thus, the salutation is important—how I address you is crucial —because I am addressing you as bearers of the tradition. I am addressing you as people who are located in Yahweh's tenting place. I am addressing you as people who intersect with particular persons and have a variety of cultural analytic perspectives of the nature of human existence. What I shall try to call you forth to be is your own people in your own places, taking seriously your tasks as, primarily, theologians.

My discipline has a pre-secular definition out of which I operate. Originally my discipline referred to helping acts done by representatives of Christ Jesus—offering healing, guiding, sustaining, and reconciling to the troubled, whose troubles arise in the context of ultimate meanings and concerns. The point of view implies that God endowed the world—the sphere of ordinary human existence—with meaning and significance to the passion, death, and resurrection of our Lord Jesus Christ, and that we are called in the places where we are at home—that is, with theological language, Scriptural stories, Scriptural meanings, narratives, truthful perceptions and through worship, liturgy, and the sacraments—to a task which is primarily one of theology. Metaphysically, every time someone comes to us, that person is asking us, "But what is true?" We are called to be metaphysicians, and every time anybody comes to us, that person is saying, "How am I to live in the middle of history?" People come to us for moral guidance, and if all we have to offer is a "TA" language and a few little technical, psychological skills, we are betraying our calling.

Thus, I want to redefine the field, to call you forth as the people who define the field and for whom it exists, rather than other people who have in the past been its primary definers. We are not academic theologians, we are not biblical scholars, we are not growth coaches, we are not sex therapists, we are not primarily assertiveness trainers; we are holy, priestly people in ecclesial places, and it is time that we take seriously what we do rather than continually try to apply what somebody else tells us to do.

Three things are important here, and I shall mention them very briefly. First, I should like to concentrate on the valuation you place on yourself and on your own ministry. I shall suggest that we look to ourselves for models and images and metaphors rather than to another discipline or to someone who is part of the Church but stands at a different place, namely, in the seminaries. Perhaps I mean to suggest that some of us are "sleepers." "Sleepers" are people who have not been discovered yet on the speaking circuit, and yet know as much about important things as those of us who are supposedly the "experts." I am interested in sleepers, those of you who somehow have kept loving priestly ministry and have discovered that every once in a while you do something right—whether through God's grace or your own. I want to uncover people like you and I want to call you forth to value that which you are about within this delicate balance one finds in being in a priestly ministry between not wanting to be elitist, but also not wanting to be egalitarian. I am not an elitist who has all the answers, but I am not just an egalitarian. I am a person who places myself in the kind of perspective which enables me to stand present with people in the middle of their histories and to help them clarify what is truthful and how they are to live.

Second, as Reinhold Niebuhr once said, "Are we really fools for Christ or simply damned fools?" And I am interested—since we are damned fools no matter what we do—in stressing that part of us which is foolish for Christ. I know that it is foolish to be in priestly ministry if one has any illusions about getting in control of existence—if one has any illusions about "bringing in the kingdom," whether in one's own culture, one's own community, or even in one's own church. We in priesthood delude ourselves if we expect people to collapse into being what we want them to be, or if we expect God to collapse into being what we would prefer God to be. For a moment I want us to risk being priestly, holy people in ecclesial places and to see what can come out of that.

Finally, then, my presentation essentially involves sharing with you a vision. The vision is of the possibility of a shift in paradigms from a therapeutic model of pastoral care and counseling to an ecclesial model of pastoral care and counseling, and from a growth group model of understanding history to a how-do-people-stand-it-in-churches-together model or paradigm of the meaning of historical existence. In describing this vision, I hope to catch you up in the task of understanding that what you do in those places is theology, not just second-rate expediency or coping as best you can. If anyone is called to be of excellence in our culture at this period of history, it is people like us as we are called to stand there at this juncture of historical existence to be ministers. It makes all the difference in the world by what paradigm you live, because it is the paradigm out of which you live that basically determines what the people are going to see in you. It is imperative that we find a different kind of paradigm than the therapeutic paradigm which has informed far too much of my discipline.

II. Foundation

This section is necessary because I felt that if I was going to attempt to redefine a whole discipline when the discipline itself might not be a familiar one, I had best give a few modest foundation remarks. The discipline of pastoral hermeneutics has turned away from people like ourselves and has become something quite different than it originally was. Let me begin with the phrase "the secularization of pastoral care," which comes from Don Browning, a professor of my discipline at the University of Chicago. I do not wish to attempt to turn back an irreversible historical clock, to let go the affirmation of the secularization processes that has informed us in our care, counseling, and therapeutic practices. What I do want is to hold on and push those developmental understandings, those dynamic understandings, the power of the emotions, the truthfulness of particular human existence; but at the same time I also want to know the problematics of a secularization of pastoral care, which have gotten in the way of us handling the Word rightly and knowing what to do with Scripture.

If you look at this field very carefully, there are four unfortunate ways in which people deal with Scripture. The first is to develop something called biblical counseling, so that whenever anybody comes in you simply quote from the Scripture. The second way, exemplified by people such as Howard Clinebell, uses the Bible without contemporary analytical or hermeneutical tools to make a psychological point that verifies the psychological point of view. In other words, one discovers that Jesus was primarily a growth coach. In our work, then, we search about for suitable Scriptural analogies showing that Jesus was basically about growth. Basically, I would argue that historically this is pretty much what has happened to us as priests. The third unfortunate way of using Scripture is to let it go completely and to not consider that it is an important resource at all. This phenomenon is typified in the AAPC and CPE training of a few years ago. Finally, the fourth way is to be intimidated by Scripture. Because you have not had the most recent course in hermeneutical interpretation, you do not feel confident to seek out what it is you can do or to trust your own disciplined, critical roots in Bible and Scripture and relate them to your pastoral practice.

The secularization of pastoral care has had a number of consequences. Most importantly, it has led us to become critical of our own persons, priesthood, places, church, and perspectives —Bible and theology—and to accept secular truth as self-evident at the same time as we automatically criticize sacred truth. There has been almost a complete reversal: anything that is secular must therefore be true, and anything that partakes of sacredness must therefore be held up to scorn. Thus we have demeaned and diminished our own calling.

The second thing that has happened is that, as a discipline which does not incorporate its own history and master its own history and development, pastoral hermeneutics is in danger of losing its sense of direction and of becoming irrelevant. Pastoral care goes back to pre-Hebrew Scripture times, and it seems that sometimes we forget that all of this marvelous history through centuries of people caring with people happened, believe it or not, prior to Freud. To be able to look back and pick up on some of the magnificence of our own tradition might enable us to save ourselves from being silly, repetitious, boring, and banal —which, if one wishes to go out and read in the discipline of pastoral counseling and pastoral care, are precisely the qualities one so often finds in the literature. Many of us use it just as if we did not know any better, because we do not value our own calling or work out of our own places and our own commitments to develop a literature that expresses who we are and who we are called to be.

Philip Reiff, who has written major critiques of psychoanalysis, has said, "Basically, the training of psychoanalysts and the training of clergy have meant we are training boring people." I think he is right on both counts, and many of us are boring because we sometimes act with so little imagination that I could almost see some of us referring Mr. and Mrs. Othello to a marriage counselor, or sending Iago off to a work camp or a weekend sensitivity group. We sometimes respond to the kinds of people who come to us with the trivialities of psychology gone wild (and I am not here denigrating the importance of psychology, rather only attempting to provide a corrective to that discipline in our own areas).

Another thing that Reiff says in his critique of Freud is that, "What happens to psychoanalysts after Freud was that instead of writing papers called 'On a Theme Suggested by One of My Patients,' they started to write papers called 'On a Patient Suggested by One of My Themes'." I think we do that all the time. We see a theme and we try to look at a person out of it, instead of standing present with the wonder and the otherness of those people who come to us to learn how to live in history, to learn what is truthful.

The third thing that has happened is that we tend to turn to others who are supposedly more highly valued than ourselves, for I believe many of us in priestly ministry basically view ourselves as second-rate. We think we are second-rate academic theologians, and therefore we do not claim to be theologians at all. We think we are second-rate psychiatrists and therefore we do not claim to be priests and pastors. We think we are second-rate biblical scholars and therefore we do not claim to use Scripture or let it speak out of our lives. We do not want to be fundamentalists, so when people come to us hungry for the Word and a paradigm to bring them meaning and truth in their existence, we put on a front of decorum and control that hides our lack of confidence to respond meaningfully to their needs.

I want us to shift from a therapeutic to an ecclesial model, and in doing so there would be a difference in some of the criteria by which we perceive our work. In a therapeutic model a person has a one-dimensional experience with the therapist. In our model—the ecclesial one—we have multi-dimensional relationships with the people with whom we minister. We see them at dinners, we offer them the sacrament, they hear us preach, we run into them in the streets. Sometimes we know more about their lives than we want to know, and, however you want to put it, we are stuck with them. This is not the same as the therapeutic model, where we see them for an hour a week in an office. That model does not fit our setting. It is the right model for a therapist, but not for us. We do not have our people for an hour a week in an office; we hustle and bustle with them. Psychiatrists are lucky, because the people who go to them go away; but our people do not go away—they keep hanging around. The literature suggests that this is a tremendous problem, instead of the most marvelous asset of living with people in history that we have as one of the major gifts of priesthood.

The second major difference between the two models is that psychiatrists do not have to make public statements on issues, such as where they stand on the ordination of women, prayer books, or homosexuality. They have the luxury of silence on issues that hurt. We do not. We preach, and, one would hope, occasionally we can say something that makes someone angry or we state a hermeneutic of suspicion that calls someone to task. Those are the same people with whom we counsel and care. It is a different dynamic, and therefore it is a different model we need to be developing. How do you do care and counseling where you are both public and private? How do you relate to people out of that kind of a dimension?

The third difference is that we have special opportunities of our place and our persons that therapists do not have. We can take initiative; we can reach out to people; we have available resources of Scripture, of story, of narrative, of ways of seeing. What happened as we took over psychological techniques, which we desperately needed and continue to use as very valuable tools, is that we also took over psychological points of view which gradually diminished our own.

I believe we could get very angry with theologians if we wanted to do so, because I basically believe that theologians abandoned us and made of theology something done only in seminaries and in the writing of books, instead of an activity of Christian community. Theology properly belongs in our parishes. It properly belongs in a place where we invite theologians to share with us and our people an interpretation of existence and of how to understand the nature of God and of how to live in a truthful way. The precise issues of scholarship have a place there too, but in terms of *praxis*—as put into practice with issues and problems which arise. This form of theology predates the other, and it is time for us to claim it back, because this theology is also the source of what it means to be in pastoral care and counseling in the 1980's.

In terms of paradigms, which I mentioned earlier, I am interested in shifting the paradigm from growth group to Christian community. Paradigms I define, like Kuhn, as "a theoretical formulation that is broad enough to organize a wide diversity of existing data into an internally consistent and coherent body of knowledge." I want to shift those of us in pastoral care and counseling away from the growth group paradigm to the paradigm of Christian community. I shall, however, mention just a few things about the growth group paradigm, because growth groups (and I am, myself, involved in them within my own pastoral counseling) are useful in certain situations, although there are some unfortunate consequences arising from their use. The growth group paradigm tends to emphasize the self; it tends to teach a person that he or she can will existence; it tends to be a short-term being-together, where people can love and hug each other a lot, but not have to stand each other in the midst of ordinary existence. Thus, for the growth group paradigm to be meaningful and truly helpful, one must use it in such a way so as to enable people to learn how to stand each other better.

The paradigm of Christian community, in ecclesia, is a much different, and more historically prevalent, paradigm. There is a center in Christian community in ecclesia that somehow holds us together through our differences—with the battles over time—so that we learn how to stand each other. I do not understand the basic question of Christian existence as bringing forth the kingdom in your local parish. I understand that, at best, what we are doing is helping the people stand each other so that they can find in their midst, this side of the Promised Land, the kind of hopefulness that lets them keep believing that the Promised Land is over there.

This is a different atmosphere in which to do pastoral care and counseling from one where the understanding of community contains no sense of a center that holds us together over time. In our paradigm of ecclesial community there is a value placed on staying together, and also on living an ordinary existence over time, on finding the liminal and the radiant in the midst of that ordinary existence—not by leaving it and searching for it elsewhere—and, above all, on a sense of otherness. In Christian community, we encounter real otherness. There are different points of view. We do not all collapse into people who are just alike.

How do pastoral care and pastoral counseling deal with this kind of reality? In our paradigm—shifting from therapeutic to ecclesial, from growth group to Christian community—people do not come to us for techniques of existence, although that may be a part of what we offer (and we should be excellent in that area, so that our lack of technical competence does not get in the way). The technical competence is just the preliminary, because those people come to us looking for a center, for meaning, for interpretation of history, for a sense of truth and how to live; and they come to us because they are so naive as to believe we have something to offer. They come to us out of a hope that we are there, living out of a paradigm that has something to say to them. Yet, so often, if we do not have that passion or that belief or that sense of hope that is not wish, we leave them empty.

We are about in pastoral ministry the matter of "existence clarification," which, obviously, is quite a profound undertaking. There is a group of people in this culture which is called upon by other people to help them clarify the nature of existence, and we are that group. We are about the only people in this kind of calling—the only ones who can take that task upon ourselves and can discipline ourselves to be the kind of person capable of performing it successfully. Therefore, we are called to be about pastoral hermeneutics, the interpretation of historical existence.

First, however, I should like briefly to differentiate pastoral hermeneutics from the hermeneutics of suspicion and the hermeneutics of disclosure. What I mean by the hermeneutics of suspicion is the kind of work that Mary Daly, working with feminist categories, does in questioning the basic structure of reality itself in terms of the ordering of the sexes. The hermeneutics of suspicion is also essentially what characterizes the work of Darwin and Freud. Freud made us understand that we are not just rational beings, and in making us aware of the existence of the unconscious, he opened up a whole new way of understanding the self-evidents of the world. Similarly, Darwin offered us a whole new understanding of the sense of our organic basis. In a sense, these approaches characterize basically what the Christian faith is—a calling to terms of the self-evident ways by which people understand the world.

When I refer to the hermeneutics of disclosure, I am thinking of the work done by people like Carter Hayward, Phyllis Trible, Eleanor McLaughlin, and others who lift up and disclose alternative models, such as the dance as a paradigm. Also, I think of the focusing upon the women in Scripture, whom we have previously ignored, in order to disclose a sense of that otherness which allows us new ways to see and new ways to be.

I am interested in both of these kinds of hermeneutics, but at this period of my life I am primarily interested in a pastoral hermeneutics, which has to do with people like ourselves living in the midst of history, informed by a whole tradition of which we are the bearers, nurtured by all the various paths of cultural analytics, daring and risking to stand present with a particular person at a particular period of his or her life. The key aspect which differentiates pastoral hermeneutics from a hermeneutics of disclosure or a hermeneutics of suspicion is the particularity of the task. We are always stuck with Mr. Jones himself. There is no universal human sitting there in the office. We can "get by," if we wish, by readjusting the self-evidents in terms of universal human categories, or by lifting up a whole model of varieties of disclosure to draw upon, but in our situation we are always stuck with particular people at a particular point of their lives, needing a particular biblical meaning and truthful interpretation relevant to the present moment.

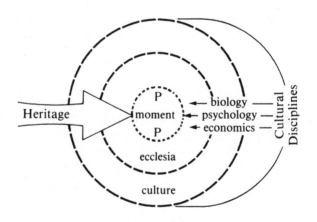

III. Interpretation

I shall begin this section with a brief explanation of the diagram, above. The small circle in the middle represents the relationship between priest and another person, while the broader circle around represents the ecclesial community. In the small circle, we could write in a "P" and a "P", denoting a pastor and a person. Behind each of these there might be other people, because sometimes the pastoral moment involves us with more than one other person, or even with people not in ecclesial community but in the broader community—in the whole culture. Here, however, let us be concerned with the pastoral moment in ecclesial community. Thus, we have priest, the other person who has come to him or her, and, in addition, other people in close proximity, which is important because one of our tasks, as different from the therapist, is to call forth our laity to be caring people with each other and to educate and train them to do pastoral kinds of tasks.

On the left side of the diagram there is a large arrow pointing in towards the center, and this arrow represents our whole tradition and heritage: Scripture, theology, spiritual background, the residue of everything learned in seminary, the articles we read (or do not have time to read) in various journals, etc. Also, one would hope, the arrow represents our prayer life, our reflective life, our meditative life—that part that nurtures and informs us as holy person, as priest.

The crescent-shaped segment on the right side of the diagram represents the cultural analytics which are also available for our use. The longest arrow coming into the middle of the pastoral moment represents psychology, longest because what we tend to have done is to have selected one cultural discipline, namely psychology, and defined all of pastoral practice around it, which is quite all right to do, as long as we remember there are other "arrows"). The other, smaller arrows in the diagram represent other disciplines and areas of study about which I think, perhaps, we should be learning something—for example, economics or cultural anthropology or biology, all of which we speak about as if we knew something when we actually have never made any disciplined, systematic study of these fields at all. Somehow in this interpretive scheme, psychology has come to overshadow and preclude all these other disciplines and fields.

However, I am most concerned here with making us aware that we need to strengthen the theology side to have it be more weighted in looking at this moment. We do need to know what elements we have chosen to draw upon from the cultural side so that we do not confuse what we are about in this unique priestly moment in our own holy place with what someone else is doing in some other place where the use of those other elements and disciplines may be perfectly appropriate.

The pastoral moment, then is inevitably interpretive. We are helping everyone who comes to us to interpret existence. It is inevitably creative. We must not make it a derivational moment. We are the ones who are there as the creators of what is going to be said. Through us pass all of what the arrows in the diagram represent and all of the various analytics which are available to us, so that somehow our mouths open and we say something or do something in that moment to reach out and touch the other person. The pastoral moment prepares us to be able to do precisely that at that moment which is what I understand my discipline is all about.

This pastoral moment, then, is really invitational. We are inviting that person to understand existence. It is not an announcement that says, "I know what it is, here it is." It is a creative moment, not a technical one. Everyone who is just out of seminary experiences the kind of dread in facing the pastoral moment which makes one hastily think back over all the textbooks in order to answer the question. "What should I say now?" However, most of us now are far beyond that point, yet still we do not trust ourselves—our own resources, our own background, and our sense of what works and what does not. And yet this is precisely what we need to do. The pastoral moment is a creative moment, and it is a theological moment. It is not primarily a psychological moment—not an expression of the universal human—but a particular moment. Finally, for those of us in pastoral ministry, it is a cumulative moment, not a one-shot deal. When one is in a parish there is the marvelous opportunity of having time with people—seeing them over time—and from that opportunity a cumulative, meaningful, historical relationship may be able to emerge.

There are problems to be overcome in utilizing all the opportunities offered in the pastoral moment, and in my discipline they may be characterized as methodological problems. The methodological problem of pastoral care concerns us at that intersection, at that juncture of history, when we attempt to offer an interpretation of existence. This is a serious methodological problem, because there are so many different factors to account for: the factor of ourselves—why we are there and whether we have a faithful position or not; the necessity for some sort of an analysis of the other person—all the historical knowledge we have about them; and the choice of which dimension from the tradition should be selected—how does the Scripture come to bear on this moment and which of the available cultural dimensions should be used. Some experts in my discipline see the methodological problem of pastoral care as the most crucial theological issue of the present-day church, yet it is not the experts but the ordained ministry who are left to work out this methodological problem. Earlier it was mentioned that the pastoral moment is an invitational moment directed towards the other person, but it is also an invitation to us to see the compelling excitement of our task.

What are some of the ways in which we can make use of this invitation? Taking "methodology" down to a more particular, more basic, and, it is to be hoped, more useful level, I offer the following suggestions under three headings, or three areas to which we should pay greater attention.

1. Particularity in Narrative

In our own parishes, we encounter people whose stories are not the kind which appear in the literature or in the case histories. This is the kind of experience, taken from our own pastoral lives, which we need to use as the basis of metaphor and example in our counseling and care. Every pastor has brave, courageous people in his or her parish who embody something about how to live in history, yet these people do not appear in the textbooks. Under this story-way of looking at existence, if we are deeply rooted in the Gospel, we find ways in which the stories there have a great deal of truthfulness about what it means to live this side of the Promised Land with the hope of the Promised Land coming. I believe that most pastors know this, but then they read a technical, psychological approach and start acting as if the human was self-defining, self-assertive, and was not inevitably bound in relationships with other people. The point is to reflect seriously on the meaning of people's stories.

2. Wonder and Otherness

Once we allow our people's stories to disclose themselves— not as case histories, but as persons struggling to find meaning in existence—we shall begin to discover real differences among them.

Whenever we start listening to people's stories, we begin to discover in them the otherness of our people, and we come to experience wonder in looking at our people. We begin to ask ourselves how we can join them, instead of remaining aloof and objectively apart in attempting what we try to do in many of our psychological disciplines, which is to collapse them into each other so that they are all the same. This is the reason why biblical narratives and biblical points of view which contradict each other are so truthful to the nature of human existence and to the way in which pastors see that nature in their parishes. I am interested in pastoral experiences that reflect the ways in which we help others to understand otherness, and through that recognition of otherness hold alive the sense of the otherness of God at whom we can still wonder and before whom we can still bow with a sense of ministry rather than with a technical competence, because we are concerned with the lives of our people as they disclose themselves.

3. Pastoral Excellence and Holy Hunches

The phrase "holy hunches" is one I have borrowed from a publication of the St. Alban's Institute. What I mean by that is simply the recognition that every once in a while we seem to do something right—that we experience a "hermeneutical moment," in which at some given moment what we said seemed to address the spiritualness, the theology of the moment, and that we were truly present with the other person. Through our experience, and especially through our mistakes, we have built up numerous ways in which we have learned to trust our own judgment. What I am saying is we should not let the literature get in the way of our trust of ourselves, because much of that literature was not written for us in our places.

Under this rubric of "holy hunches," there are three things on which I would like to see all of us concentrate. The first involves an awareness of how different "transference" is within the dimension of pastoral experience as compared with that of the therapeutic relationship. Transference is something of crucial importance, and it takes a different form when you are with somebody for an hour a week in a therapy situation, where the concept of transference may be the central phenomenon. Strange things, however, happen to transference in the multi-dimensional relationships of pastors and people.

An awareness of this leads to my second point, which concerns an understanding of what friendship means in parish life. The literature suggests you should not have friends in the parish. While in some clearly recognizable situations, friendship may not be the appropriate form of relationship in meeting certain people's needs, I have never known any healthy pastors and priests who did not have friends in the parish. I would like to see people, like ourselves, who have risked having friends in the parish because we are called to be sisters and brothers together, not be identified or to identify others in terms of genital sexuality, but rather in terms of something called friendship and Christian community.

Third, I am interested in seeing us bring forth out of our parishes some literature that differentiates between "wishing" and "hoping." Wishing is of the nature of "I wish that tomorrow the world situation would stabilize," which is distinct from the hoping of Paul when he says, "Now I see through a glass darkly, but then I shall see face to face." Concluding my emphasis on being aware of our holy hunches and pastoral excellence, I suggest that there are ways in which understanding how people's religion informs, sustains, guides, and nurtures them helps us to understand them psychologically, rather than always using the psychological categories to help us define the religious experience.

IV. Implication

Here I wish to begin by charging us to take ourselves more seriously and to think of ourselves as holy persons in an ecclesial place called forth to interpret the nature of existence. Whether we like it or not, people are always coming to us to ask us questions such as, "What is true?" "How can I live in history?" "By what moral structure should I live?" Our call is to take ourselves and history seriously. By taking history seriously, I mean taking our places seriously and not trying to will a different existence or to leap out of history into a Promised Land that we create, instead of learning how to live with grace and dignity this side of the Promised Land with the hope of the Promised Land.

If we are able to do this, we shall have things to say about the nature of history, the nature of community, and the nature of otherness, which theologians in academic communities are looking for. We shall understand that many times community is standing one another over time, rather than calling forth the perfect community. We shall understand that there is an otherness where people do not collapse into being just the same, but where they have to learn how to negotiate existence around otherness. Finally, we shall understand that history is a very ambiguous place, a kaleidoscope, a maze of events, to which we seek to bring a measure of intelligibility through the perspectiveness of the Gospel and of our tradition—a tradition which offers us a way to see what history means, because it provides us with a particular understanding of the nature of God, who joins us into history and brings us the grace and dignity to sustain ourselves and to not give up the vision.

What presences and what resources do we possess for meeting our task? First, I would suggest that we have to start seeing the issue, and if we could simply see that this very basic prerequisite is indeed exactly what we are called upon to do in our ministry, we could then create a whole new literature together that would come out of an ecclesial understanding of pastoral care and counseling that would have something to do with sacraments. The sacraments themselves should be taught, for surely sacramental theology has something to do with pastoral care. The power of the sacraments is not a technique one manipulates; rather, the power resides in the relationship and the care and the presence one shares when one possesses the special kind of calling of the ministry. Yet, there is almost no literature on sacramental worship and liturgy and its relationships to the particularity of pastoral practices.

What other resources do we have? I would suggest ourselves, and in this I would call us forth to take seriously all those points that hurt in our own places and also to define those resources of faith which sustain us there, because the paradigm which we live is the one which our people will see. How do you care for yourself? How do you care for each other? Are there places where priests can learn to trust each other? I am convinced that one of the reasons we are not theologians at these junctures of history, interpreting existence, is because we do not always have a faithful enough reservoir to draw upon which would allow us to stand it at those junctures. If we cannot stand it there, then we withdraw and, in doing so, we implicitly invite other people to withdraw as well. Who are we, then, to be? Foolish ones, certainly, to take on such responsibilities. But, at least, God's foolish ones.

Narrative and Symbol:
Key to New Testament Spiritualities

David W. Tracy*

In this paper I shall be concerned with a theological use of some principles from contemporary hermeneutics and literary criticism. The emphasis will be on narrative in the New Testament, what that might disclose in terms of religious and theological realities, and the relationship of distinct kinds of theological languages, namely, Paul and John, to the originating symbols.

It is not necessary to decide between proclamation as a genre and narrative as the primary New Testament genre. The New Testament, in fact, includes and demands both. So it would seem does human experience. There is something in experience which we all know seems to demand story or narrative. In part, I suspect, narrative alone provides us with some fuller way to order and unify our actual lived experience—with its tensions and surprises, its reversals and triumphs, its experience through memory of a real past and to anticipation and hope of a real future in the tensed unity of every, ever-vanishing "now" of the present.

Each of us knows that the stories persons tell us disclose their character to us far more than their theories. The unique story each person is discloses a human possibility that might otherwise

*David Tracy is Professor of Theology in the Divinity School at the University of Chicago. He is the author of several works, including the critically-acclaimed A BLESSED RAGE FOR ORDER. *A slightly different version of Professor Tracy's address reproduced here will appear in his forthcoming book,* THE ANALOGICAL IMAGINATION, *to be published by Crossroads in 1981.*

go unremarked. The classic stories disclose the meaning of a life actually lived in the grip of some classic human possibility—the lived actuality of hope, tragedy, resignation, fulfillment, or the struggle for justice or love. The particular focus of the fundamental existential questions in our situation often receive far more disclosure from some classic story: the story of how a single human being lives and faces death, as distinct from philosophical or theological reflections upon mortality; a classic story disclosing Hubris and Nemesis, as distinct from ethical reflections upon finitude; a classic story disclosing the reality, the lived reality, of the utopian world vision, as distinct from sociological reflections upon ideologies and utopias.

The Gospels share the prejudice of life itself, a story as a key to lived experience. They share the assumption common to humankind that life itself has the character of a story. The Gospels emerge from a response to the event of proclamations that Jesus, the crucified Messiah, is risen and vindicated by God, only to submerge themselves in retelling the story of this Jesus, the proclaimer of God's reign in word and deed, the Crucified and Risen One, now experienced and confessed by the community as present to them as Lord and Christ. Here proclamation as a word of address confronts us directly with its word of address and its powerful appeal to respond to that kind of unsettling word, the nearness of God disclosed in this event of Jesus Christ. The Gospels prefer, unlike Paul, for example, who emphasizes proclamation, to tell the story of this Jesus and to allow this narrative's disclosive power to work its eventful disclosure and transformation.

The Gospels remain, of course, proclaiming, confessing narratives, and yet they remain narratives. With our emphasis on proclamation, we too often forget that they are narratives whose classic religious power is not separable, I believe, from the narrative form itself. In the Gospels the event of proclamation comes to expression as narrative.

The genre gospel, unique, it seems, to Christianity, is a complex genre whose exact nature is still debated among experts. Yet, at the very least, the gospel is a complex structure containing several narratives. There is the miniature gospel, so called, of individual sayings about Jesus or attributed to Jesus, which make grace and deliverance visible through retelling typical episodes and anecdotes. Then, of course, there are the narratives *par excellence* of Jesus himself, the parables, recently reinterpreted by literary and hermeneutical thinkers, as the paradigmatic Jesuanic discourse of what the reign of God is really like. That reign is like what happens in these unsettling, these jarring stories where metaphorical disclosure takes a narrative form. Also, we have the narratives of the deeds of Jesus in his ministry—those deeds which express in action as they are told the coming of God's reign proclaimed in word, as well as those deeds for the outcast and the oppressed. Then there are those strange and convention-shattering narratives of his table fellowship with tax collectors and sinners and his overturning of the moneychangers in the temple.

However, above all, there remains, of course, the key narratives in the Christian Gospel, the Passion narratives. Martin Kähler, I admit, may well have exaggerated the matter when he made his famous statement on the Gospel of Mark, that the Gospel is a Passion narrative with an extended introduction. Yet, whatever the exegetical exaggeration in those remarks, they bear a mark of theological truth, for in the Passion narratives the heart of the Christian story about Jesus—the main plot, if you will—can be found. What is the nature of a story which its community chooses to confess its faith—the story of the Crucified and Risen One—and chooses to tell the story of the rejection and crucifixion of this Jesus—the proclaimer of the kingdom of God—now proclaimed in the other genre of proclamation itself as Jesus the Christ?

The Passion narrative is set in the context of the proclamation of the real presence of God to the present community and their experience of the Spirit, but the story is set, as well, in the context of that larger story of deliverance of the covenanted people, Israel. It is not only that a reader cannot understand the concepts —covenant, deliverance, law and prophecy, suffering Messiah and apocalyptic hope, promise and fulfillment, wisdom and confession—of the New Testament without the enveloping context of the Old Testament, but it is also the case that the story of Jesus confessed and narrated in these Gospels finds its basic presuppositions, its larger context, in the story of promise and fulfillment, covenant and creation, nearness to the God of Israel and Israel's deliverance, in the texts of confession and narrative, of law and prophecy, of the genres of hymn, of wisdom, and of apocalyptic, in the Old Testament.

However, there is a singular difference here in the New Testament: whereas in the Old Testament the narrative as narrative ranges over the long history of the entire people Israel, in the New Testament the entire weight of this story of deliverance is concentrated upon the single individual Jesus of Nazareth. Here is the story of the ministry and deeds, words, actions, passion and resurrection, of a single man who focuses the entire plot of the story and seems to disclose the meaning of all the other subplots told in the story.

The present reality of the Christ to the community seems to free Mark, for example, to develop a narrative which is like an apocalyptic drama as a narrative, whereby this Jesus is the apocalyptic Son of Man whose messianic secret discloses the necessity somehow in the story itself for a suffering Messiah. The experience of his present reality seems to free Luke and Matthew to develop distinct kinds of narratives of this same Jesus, and would serve, as Norman Perrin has suggested, as foundation myth stories for the later community experiencing and witnessing to his present reality among them. The presence of the narrative form, I suggest, allows even John to prevent his theological meditations, his imagery and symbols, from escaping from their intrinsic connection to the person Jesus, remembered and confessed as logos through a narrative.

The narratives find different ways to unfold the character of who this Jesus is in the plot of the story. His strength and weakness, the active and redemptive suffering and love of this character, is disclosed—from the incognito character, the suffering Son of Man, in Mark; through the more open yet, for me at least, still reticent visibility of the character Jesus in Luke and Matthew; to the sheer manifestation of the lifting up in the Cross as Jesus' heroic, active exaltation in John. The authority of the person told of in these stories is startling. It is both like and unlike that of the stories of the prophets, for the reign of God is not only proclaimed in parable, proverb, and eschatological saying on his own authority, but is narrated as happening even now in the deeds of Jesus: his willingness to flout both social convention and law where he sees fit; his prophetic insistence upon openness to the poor, the oppressed, the sick, the outcast; his signs of manifestation; his exorcisms; his cures and miracles; his prayer of intimacy to the Father as Abba. His actions, in sum, in this narrative are like a prophet, yet one who assumes an unprophet-like authority of his own—grounding in a seemingly shocking intimacy with God.

When we approach these familiar, perhaps all too familiar, narratives as narratives, with the aid of literary, critical, and hermeneutical methods, as many critics are doing today, we may, I think, have some chance to perceive anew some of the religious and theological significance of these stories. We can do this by perceiving the dangerous memory of Jesus in the form that best reveals it—the narratives of a person, a life, which discloses through its own narrative form what life can and should be. These narratives, moreover, maintain the same tensive character of the founding symbols, Cross and Resurrection, of the original proclamation—and, as I shall suggest shortly, of later theologies —through their frequent strategies of surprise and shock in what might be called intensification procedures—of proverb, parable, and eschatological saying; and in their portrayal of the shocking fitness of this Jesus in an anger which is at once a compassion, a weakness which is also a strength, and a love which is also judgment.

These narratives, moreover, end in the transformation of the event of the resurrection, the event of vindication, disclosing the true significance of the Cross, while Cross and Resurrection together show the significance in the narratives of the whole ministry of deed and word. Yet, still the reader cannot avoid noticing, I think, that as narratives, these narratives do not really end, especially in Mark (a phenomenon that the literary critic Frank Kermode has pointed out in his recent discussion of the genesis of secrecy in Mark). Even in Luke-Acts, the story seems to go on into an open future for all whose reality has already been disclosed in the narrative proleptically. Attention pervades these narratives as narratives, between a fulfillment of the eschatological reign of God in the ministry, Passion, and Resurrection, and the as yet unfulfilled hope for the end time, for all the living and the dead. Above all, the eschatological symbols in this narrative, almost as a minefield, seem to me to disclose this "not yet" character in the narrative itself, a story which ends in the incredible paradoxical triumph of Cross and Resurrection and begins in that ending its movement to all; it does not end.

The prophets and apocalyptic-minded among us are likely to resonate, for example, to one temporary end in the story of the Crucified One—the frightening, shaking, "not yet" cry of Jesus in Matthew and especially in Mark: "My God, my God, why have you forsaken me?" The more ordinary Christian, a type which, let us remember, the Gospel also honors and for whom it demands that attention must be paid, is more likely to overhear the narrative in Luke and the trusting words of Luke's Jesus: "Father, into your hands I commend my spirit." Others in the Christian community who read these narratives—such as the contemplatives and mystics, and all those who honor the religious manifestations of the cosmos from chaos—are more likely, I think, to turn to the narratives of John's exalted as Crucified One and his final words: "It is accomplished."

Yet, despite whatever classic root of spirituality any individual Christian takes in trying to live a life like that narrated in these narratives, no one reader can forget that the story must finally be remembered in its entirety and its diversity as a whole, of real negation and real exaltation, of real suffering and active love; as a proclamation and manifestation of the Crucified and Risen One who lived, lives, and will live; as a story which discloses the shocking truth that the final power with which we all must deal is not the coercive power of this world or our own tortured memories, but the power of that pure, unbounded, compassionate, and judging love which is the final reality, who is God.

The Christian story has not ended and will not end, if we note these narratives, until all the living and the dead are touched. The story discloses the tense reality of both a real "always already" presence among us, and yet throughout a real "not yet" and negation of the present. It discloses the individual as a real individual, called to that individuality, and yet at the same time as related to all, as in the "non-end" of the narrative. This story disallows, as story, any assumption that the reality of the "not yet" is not as real as the "always already" presence of God in creation, covenant, and Jesus Christ, and thereby, in the lived dialectic of Christian existence itself, portrayed in the form of these narratives.

The New Testament and the later Christian tradition turn not only to the genre's proclamation and narrative, but also to certain major tensive symbols and images—and not just to literary genres—to disclose the fuller manifestation and power of the proclaimed "that" and the narrative "what" and "who." Central among those symbols are three: Cross, Resurrection, Incarnation. Each decisively discloses some major aspect of the event of God's self-manifestation in Jesus Christ. All three disclose, as a dialectical unit of symbols, the full range and meaning of that event.

The Cross, after all, is a strange choice for a religion to choose, if one thinks of the history of religions, as its major symbol. The Cross discloses the power, pain, and seriousness of the negative, the conflict, destruction, contradiction, the suffering of love which is the reality of a life worthy of the name human. The Cross discloses God's power as a love which appears as weakness to the powers of the world. It discloses the intensified rejection incumbent upon the preaching and ministry of Jesus as told in the narratives. The Cross as symbol resonates as well to the great themes of all religious classics—the death of the present self as the way to new life, the stupidity and obtuseness of human beings when confronted by sheer goodness and courage. The Cross discloses to the Christian, I think, the suffering love of God's own self by its intensified focus on that love as the ultimate binding internal relationship of the divine and the human.

The Resurrection vindicates, confirms, and transforms that journey in and through its negations of the negations of the Cross. The Resurrection grounds Christian hope in a real future for all the living and the dead. It discloses the enabling power of that reality as here even now, indeed as the reality that is always already here, if we would but note it, the reality of incarnation.

Incarnation as symbol, the symbol that for me makes sense once one understands the symbols Cross and Resurrection first, discloses the reality of the only God there is—as here now, as here always, as here in the past, present, and future—through the decisive self-manifestation in the Cross and Resurrection. Incarnation fulfills its liberating function only in intrinsic relationship to Cross and Resurrection, and Cross and Resurrection, in turn, live together or not at all.

The heart of the Christian symbol system in employing these symbols, as with my earlier remarks on employing certain narrative forms, seems to be none other than the unbreakable dialectic of all three together—Cross, Resurrection, Incarnation—disclosing through their own internal tensions the fuller meanings of the event of Jesus Christ, just as the narrative forms in the Gospel do. These symbols, like proclamation or narration, also give rise to thought. (In the now famous words of Paul Ricoeur, ''The symbol gives rise to thought, and thought always returns to and is founded in the symbol.'')

More precisely, they give rise to the response of that critical reflective thought that we now call theological language, which is itself another peculiar form of language—not narrative, not strictly symbol, not strictly proclamation, yet still another form of language and of thought which I wish to suggest discloses yet other possibilities to the human spirit. Just as the paradigmatic proclamation is expressed in the responding witness of reflective thought in the early New Testament confessions; just as the narratives tell their story within the framework of the larger story of Israel, and the theological frameworks provided by the individual redactors; so too these symbols—Cross, Resurrection, Incarnation—give rise to thought, to the thought we call theology. The symbols may lead some theologians to respond through a liturgical language, or a theology of the Risen and Crucified One imaged as high priest in the heavenly sanctuary of Hebrews. They may lead yet other theologians to articulate a theology of the apocalyptic judge of the living and the dead as the negation of the lies, delusions, compulsions, oppressions, and terror of history itself in the Book of Revelation.

Yet before these later theologies occurred in the New Testament, and before, as well, the more stable, measured, ordered, doctrinal, and pastoral theologies of the pastoral epistles emerged, two major theologies exploded into the thought-world of the New Testament. I shall refer to these, in terms of the genre of the language, as the tensive, dialectical language of Paul as contrasted with the meditative thinking of John.

Here in Paul and John one finds theology in its own-most role, for here we find the responses to the power of that event, which are responses of modes of thinking, at once critically reflective and really participatory in the event. For some persons, even their most intense religious experience is so involved in their experience of thinking itself that the two can barely be distinguished and can never be separated. So it seems to me it was for Paul and John. For the theologian, after all, and surely John and Paul are *the* theologians of the New Testament, the experience of thinking is so intrinsic to life itself that every experience must also be experienced as thinking and every thought bears all the marks of a lived experience. The power of the event of God's self-disclosure—proclaimed in the early confessions, manifested in the experience of the Spirit to the Christian community through its sacraments and liturgy, related anew in the confessing narratives of Jesus' own ministry—become concentrated as well into the reality for Christians of certain tensive symbols: the unrelieved tension of the dialectical juxtaposition of Cross and Resurrection in Paul's theological language of the Crucified and Risen One, "We preach Jesus Christ and Him crucified"; and, in contrast, the transformative manifestation of even the Cross as exaltation and glorification and, indeed, finally sheer manifestation and radical immanence and incarnation in John's language of the logos, "And we have seen His glory."

No interpreter, I think, need claim of Paul that he had a less than robust conscience, in order to see that the very strength of Paul's thinking can be shown by observing not just his concepts but his mode of thought. For me, it is dialectical through and through, indeed a dialectic which hurls the reader about and refuses any escape from facing the sheer contradiction and, at the same time, the sheer giftedness of the stark reality of the Cross of Jesus Christ. Whether justification by grace through faith is or is not the heart of Paul's theology is of course an important, but for the moment, a secondary question. It is enough, I think, to know that the dialectical language and its theology of justification is clearly present in Paul and is coherent with the dominant strain of his thought. That strain is expressed in a dialectical language which, in attempting to express the stark reality of that Cross, moves as language back and forth through dialectical intensity after intensity to releases that never quite release of the real recognition of the Crucified as the Risen One, only to return again to face and express anew, in yet new dialectical language, the thought that cannot be thought through —that the Crucified One is the one who is risen.

Through every strategy of what I would call authentic dialectical thinking and language—what others have called, as Jungel did and Paul Ricoeur did, Paul's logic of superabundance, his language of the "so much more," the "not yet," the "as though not"—Paul impels a sensitive reader, as reader, to recognize the real negations present in every human existence by seeing them in the light of the unthinkable thought of the Cross: the conflicts, delusions, compulsions in every human heart; the conflicts and contradictions in the Christian community, in history, in the cosmos itself.

Yet for Paul, all the negations are themselves negated in his dialectics, in the "so much more" disclosed in the scandal of the Cross of the Risen One, which his thought attempts to express in language. That Cross ravages sin even now, while not yet fully conquering it. Paul will not let loose his grip upon that central symbol, that Cross, that burning symbol-event of unrelieved tension and contradiction. Indeed, he will insist that language itself must be forged to express it.

Paul's theological language, I suggest, forces a reader sensitive to language to note again and again the scandal, the folly, that he wishes to express in making of the Cross an event where our lies, fears, anxieties, compulsions, illusions and distortions, our thousand strategies ever more clever to justify ourselves, meet and finally find their defamiliarizing in their recognition of the power of God as seeming weakness, suffering, real forgiveness. Paul's language will not cease from exposing his readers pathetic or heroic or tragic attempts at self-justification, while at the same time disclosing to the reader the reality of a new self in Christ: enabled, empowered, commanded, freed to become a transformed self who is even now caught up in that power and who lives even now through that gift; a self who must live to all else with the logic of the language of "as though not"; a self who must live even to the gift in power itself with the ever-repeated acknowledgement of a real faith and of trustful obedience; a self involved in the dialectics of this language itself, of a constant self-recognition of the real and never ending "not yet" in every "even now."

For Paul, only the recognition of the power of the "even now" and the reality of the "not yet" will free the individual for the God revealed in the Cross of Jesus Christ. For then the tension disclosed in that revelation will be itself, not domesticated, but intensified as it is in the language. Only then, perhaps, will the real individual, to recall a later language, *simul justus, simul peccator*, recognize its intensified experience of the reality of the power of the gift of the Cross as enabling and commanding a faith which works through love.

For Paul, all is gift, yet gift, note, is power and command. Gift is the Cross, and what language would you have to express that paradox, other than this dialectical language of Paul? The authentic response of thought, as thought, trying to express itself in appropriate language, to that power, that gift, that contradiction, is to find some expression of thought appropriate to the dialectical reality it dares to interpret. Thought itself must learn to express these negations, this tension, this contradiction, even this release. In Paul's theology, I suggest, we find a mode of thinking, a theological language as distinct from a narrative, which is finally freed of the usual compulsions to affirm my achievements, my success, my justification, and thereby finally released into the capacity to face as thought and as language the stark, conflictual, contradictory reality of the Cross itself as commanding power, enabling gift.

Where Paul proclaims "Jesus Christ and Him crucified" through all the linguistic strategies of a finely dialectical thinking, John's language moves to a form of what I would call a more meditative thinking, fully appropriate, perhaps, to his emphases. For in John, even the symbol Cross is so united to the symbols of glorification and exaltation, that Cross itself becomes a disclosure, a manifestation, of glorification. In John, the lifting up of Jesus upon the Cross is both prefigured in John's story of the ministry, as what Raymond Brown has called the Book of Signs in chapters 1-12, only later to be figured forth in the story of the Passion and Resurrection, in the Book of Glory, chapters 13-20. To manifest this Cross itself as glory, the negative note remains in this language, but it remains as authentic way of humiliation-exaltation, but now as a way to manifest God's glory in Jesus Christ.

Behind all of this, there are well-known debates even among historians of religion, as to whether religion can come as a pure word of proclamation—as a word of address which startles and shocks, upsets a reader as word, as it did for the great neo-orthodox theologians—or whether it must come through manifestation—as, say, the Eastern Orthodox tradition or many aspects of the Catholic traditions in Christianity. By manifestation, I mean a nonlinguistic power that erupts in the cosmos or in nature, or that is expressed in icon, for example, or, as I shall try to suggest in John, in meditation, in metaphysics, in art and music. To me, what is fascinating is the difference between how language itself must cope with the two sides to this debate: does it come through proclamation and then Cross, as in Paul, and then a dialectical language is needed; or does it come principally through manifestation, and then, as with John, a language is needed which actually reflects what Heidegger and others would call meditative thinking, not dialectical thinking.

That glory shines forth, for example, in what might be called the overture of the prologue and moves on to what Amos Wilder has correctly called, I think, the sacred oratorio itself. For the narrative here in John is more like listening to Handel, that is to say, as an oratorio, than it is like the synoptics, which are more straightforward narrative story. The narrative as oratorio, in

John, unfolds through the signs in the first chapters, the signs which are manifestation-oriented, of the miracles in the great discourses. The narrative moves to interpret them and climaxes, note, in the exaltation of the lifting up of the humiliated Strong One, whose glory, the glory of God, is now fully manifest in exaltation, whose risen exalted glory manifests, incarnates, the very glory and grace of God.

In John's language, I think it can be said, that thinking, to put it in a twentieth-century way, has found here a proper mode of meditative, manifest-oriented expression for this reality of unfolding, encompassing exaltation. The shock of the beauty of that glory manifests the need for a meditative, contemplative mode of thinking—a mode common both to the contemplative traditions and mystical traditions of releasement and to the more everyday, recognized experience of the giftedness of God and life itself. This sense of sheer giftedness may perhaps be best expressed in the genre icon or in hymn, as in the great overture of the prologue. Yet the same sense this language seems to exhibit may also be expressed in the mode of authentically meditative thinking that finds even narrative an occasion now for manifestation, even Cross as expression of glory. The key is to realize that glory is a religious journey that learns to let go through a humiliation which is not weakness but the very strength of the glory of God as love. Love's strength, for John, lies in its ability to let go, to sacrifice itself for the other, to let go into a manifestation of the love of Jesus Christ, the love disclosing God's own self as love and disclosing the gift of a new self-understanding to the reader, as a self in love without restriction.

In the theological languages of John and Paul, I have suggested, to note the language is also to note something about their powers of disclosure. In both all is grace, yet in Paul's language grace is disclosed as the power of the proclaimed word of the Cross, to confront the radical negativities of each and all—all who are without excuse. In John, that grade is disclosed as the gift of manifestation, the glory of the Word who is love. That gift may be rejected by some, as it is in the Book of Signs, and yet the gift may also be accepted and re-presented in a life of humiliation-exaltation, a life that manifests that released love.

The meditative character of John's language discloses to me the kind of thinking that comes upon any thinker—and Heidegger has been most profound on this, in terms of the language—as a releasement in the very letting go, as a power not our own, a gift not by us achieved. The kind of theological language most appropriate to John's theology, I think, is that kind of meditative reflection upon, and in, images, symbols, signs, which the poet and the mystic in the Christian tradition both know. For here, even the narrative becomes manifestation in becoming like a sacred oratorio, not a usual story. Even the negative reality of Cross becomes a manifestation of glory and grace. Even the stark contrasts pervading the Gospel, both as narrative and as symbol—light-darkness, truth-falsehood, life-death, faith-unfaith—become, as it were, contrapuntal themes manifesting the fuller sacramental reality of bread, water, wine—the fuller contemplative meaning in the great discourses. To me this is the pervasive, haunting, falling and rising melody of exaltation-humiliation in the entire narrative, which produces the final harmony in the language of an oratorio, where Cross itself is lifting up, disclosing the release of glory.

Throughout John's gospel the reader may hear as one hears, not words so much, but music, the reality of the pure giftedness of love as utterly self-giving. The music seems itself to yield to shift genres, to something like an icon, as that love becomes some ultimate manifestation of who God is and who we are called and enabled to be. The theological language of John—meditative, contemplative, manifestation-oriented, love-intoxicated—is the kind of thinking of releasement, of letting go, that provides its own kind of scandal, its own kind of folly—the kind of folly which fools, clowns, mystics, artists, and lovers understand. It is the kind of discourse which, even as discourse, could be characterized by what Augustine said so perfectly about it, "Give me a lover to read this text and he will understand."

It is not, however, the case that we find in Paul only the reality of proclamation and in John only the reality of manifestation. John's manifestation, after all, is one grounded in the Word. Paul's proclamation finds its final releasement in his manifestation of what it means to live in Christ. The texts of the later Pauline school, especially Ephesians and Colossians, expand that manifestation power of living in Christ to the whole cosmos, groaning to be free. Note, for example, how even contemporary writers all appeal to certain aspects, even certain languages. Teilhard de Chardin, to my knowledge, always appealed to Ephesians and Colossians, never Romans. John's manifestations and signs and symbols retain, it is true, only a muted but real future, not yet, note, in the context of their overwhelmingly realized manifesting character. Yet, that strange and provocative product of the Johannine school, the Book of Revelation, employs its own set of disturbing manifesting symbols, signs, and images to disclose perhaps the presence of a shocking, intensified "not yet" in the heart of the Johannine tradition.

In this interwoven complex of different genres of the New Testament, I believe a theologian finds the surest clues to some relatively adequate expression of the event that is disclosed in all these genres. We need proclamation, I think, to be hurled at us "often like a stone," in the famous words of Karl Barth, especially perhaps in a time much like that characterized by E. M. Forster, when he spoke of "poor, chatty little Christianity," where the very power of word is often lost. Proclamation, as in the case of Barth's early, expressionist language, as distinct from his later, dialectical language, is exactly the kind of language needed at this cultural moment to capture again the power of a proclaimed word—to shake and to upset. We need the narratives, we need proclamation, for its power to show that the event occurs even now. We need the narratives to shape the "what" as the story of this Jesus proclaimed in a manner faithful to our own experience of the story-like character of life itself, with its tensions and surprises, its shocks and achievements, its disclosures of authentic and inauthentic life.

We find the focus of New Testament disclosures and the confessing narrations in this single individual—this strange, authoritative Jesus, who proclaims God's reign in words which confront our ordinary modes of apprehension; who acts in the narrative in word and deed with a freedom and a sometimes harsh love which commands the attention of his contemporaries and of us; who dies in the narrative disgrace with the disgusting death reserved for society's rejects, while the Pilates die in their beds; who is yet raised by God and vindicated as the one who is God's own; who discloses in the narrative what an authentic life might be to all who can hear that story, and in hearing it, might join their plot entrusting hope to the "non-end" of this strange narrative. That "non-end" discloses that all, in one sense, has already happened, and yet the story has not ended, does not end. There remains in that "non-end" to the story of Jesus in the New Testament the "not yet" of each individual Christian's never-ending decisions for or against allowing the empowering plot and character of the story to become one's own story—however ordinary our own personal subplot may be, like Peter's in the narratives of the New Testament or however extraordinary, even heroic, our character might be, like Paul's in Luke-Acts.

The narratives, in turn, disclose those tensive symbols which focus the meaning and truth of that event, but now in images which disclose and transform the language anew—Cross, Resurrection, Incarnation—to the self who has already recognized that we find ourselves most surely, not through our own achievements, but through and in the classic signs and symbols scattered in our world. For the Christian, these symbols—the stark contradictory power of the Cross, the transformative hope of Resurrection, and what T. S. Eliot called "the hint half-guessed, the gift half-understood" of Incarnation—give rise among the thinkers of that community to various new forms of language called theologies.

In the sustained, even unrelieved dialectical tension of the language of Paul's theology, the sheer conflict and contradiction of the Cross is hurled in that language at all human attempts at self-sufficiency, and, thereby, as language, it can break through our usual defenses to disclose its graced scandal. In the meditative releasement of John's language, the symbols of glorification allow the reader to sense the "already" reality of existence itself as sheer gift, indeed to sense the "always already" reality of God's gracious presence in and to each and all, through history and its drive to justice and through nature and its manifestations of power. This is true, as well, in contemporary theology. Notice, for example, that in Karl Rahner's theology the emphasis is always on the "always already," and he turns to John as much as possible. Or consider F. D. Maurice or Schleiermacher or Hegel. On the other side, there are contrasting theologies, especially Bultmann's which is explicitly negative dialectical, or Hans Küng, who never uses the expressions "the always already," or "the not yet," but always speaks of "the not yet, but even now," and wishes to have his language related far more to language like Paul's.

The full complexity of these symbols and these modes of thinking—Cross, Resurrection, Incarnation, dialectics, and meditative thinking—discloses the reality of an event which is here even now, which in fact, I believe, has "always already" been here and which is still "not yet here." The dialectics of these symbols, as language, is an adverbial dialectic of an "always already" which is "yet and not yet." Only when all Christological thinking functions as a new interpretated response to those symbols; only when those symbols find the identity of who the Crucified and Risen One is in the Gospel narratives of Jesus' life, ministry, death, and resurrection; only perhaps when the narratives themselves function as both story and confession, both manifestation of the symbols and new narrative proclamation of the original act of proclamation; only perhaps when we take more seriously the genres and their clues to the worlds disclosed by these texts; only then will the full actuality of the event of Jesus Christ witnessed to in all these genres, all these images, all these modes of expression, find again in our own time some new language to reexpress its meaning.

Pentecostal Economics

Jim Wallis*

By way of introduction to the themes I wish to stress in this article, I would first like to suggest that the interpretation of the Bible, the reflections from Scripture contained in this writing, do arise out of a community, or, more precisely, they grow out of a community reading the Bible in the particular historical situation which is my context. To understand me and what I shall be discussing here, it will first be necessary to have some understanding of my context.

I am part of a community of faith—ordinary people, married and single, children—who live a common life, by which we mean sharing all that we have: resources, work, calling, hopes and fears, struggles, joys and pain. We live in the inner city of Washington, where one-third of our neighbors are out of work, one-half of those who are young are unemployed, and people in the neighborhood are losing their homes. They are being displaced by "gentrification," as the experts call it, and what that really means is the back-to-the-city movement, in which people who have the wherewithal to renovate and restore the city first remove the poor to make room. What gentrification means on the street is that those who have endured years of neglect in the city now are also going to be robbed from enjoying the new focus of attention being devoted to our urban areas. In other words, our

*Jim Wallis is the Editor of SOJOURNERS MAGAZINE in Washington, D.C. In addition to being a journalist and an author (AGENDA FOR BIBLICAL PEOPLE), Mr. Wallis is an activist and a tireless organizer—serving as a member of the "Theology in the Americas" project and as a theological advisor to charismatic and evangelical communities throughout the nation.

neighbors are people whose lives have been always characterized
by being in the wrong place at the wrong time. People are sum-
marily evicted every day and left to fend for themselves on the
streets. It is a neighborhood where kids finish high school unable
to read, where women have children while they are in fact themselves still children, where kids four and five and six years old
run in packs until after midnight unattended, living off pop-tarts
and corn chips.

However, it is not just a bad place. It is also a good place,
because the people in the neighborhood, in spite of all, are very
warm and giving people. The little that they have they share, and
sharing what little you have is the only way to get by. There is a
family with eleven children who lived with us for about six
months after they were evicted, and now that they have found
their own place, it is always full of other people with no place to
go. There perhaps is a principle in that story, which has some
Biblical roots in itself, namely, "The more you have, the less
generous you become," and, conversely, "The less you have and
the closer you have been to the edge, the more willing you are to
share what you have."

Briefly, that is our local context, but there is also a broader
historical context that shapes everything we do and everything
all of you do. Simply stated, that context is characterized by the
facts that the world's peoples are poor and that the Church in
our country is rich. Those two simple facts set our context. It is
our most important context and the one that shapes every other
context of our lives. At this moment, these facts have become
more urgent. Resources are dwindling, the poor are becoming
hungrier while the appetites of the rich grow, and the power of
violence—actual and potential—escalates almost daily. This
leads us to perhaps the central, moral reality of our times, namely,
that we are ready now to "nuke" the world into oblivion to
protect our color television sets and our dishwashers.

Our context affects our community's life in every way. It
affects our evangelism, our worship, our pastoral care, and our
theology. It has also affected our reading of the Bible. We have
reached the conclusion that the God of the Bible is on the side of
the poor, which is to say, God has a class bias. If that is not clear

from the Scriptures, then I find nothing in all of the Scriptures that is clear. That God is on the side of the poor must be elevated to the status of doctrine in a Church whose faith has been choked by its wealth and its comfort.

Thus, I wish to make a central proposition, which is that the worship of the Church has no power when that Church is invisible in the world. Peter, a simple fisherman who became an apostle, when writing to some of the earliest Christians, said, "Always be ready to give reason for the faith and the hope that is within you," which is to say, "Always be ready to explain yourself." The question that tests the power of our worship today is simply, "What do we have to explain to the world around us about the way that we live?"

When Peter told the earliest Christians, "Always be ready to give reason for the faith and hope that is within you," he was assuming something there between the lines, yet something that we dare not miss. He was assuming that a question was being asked of the early Christians by the society in which they lived, and the question goes something like this: "Why do you people live the way that you do? What causes this behavior on your part? The way that you think, the way that you act, the way that you live is something that for us is unexplainable. It seems unreasonable; it seems irresponsible. It is something we just cannot understand; it seems contrary to the way that we define our interests. It seems contrary to the way that our society, our culture, defines its interests, and it is clear that it is contrary to the way that our government defines its interests. Why do you people live this way?" Peter, recognizing the question would be asked, tells them to be ready, when the question is asked, to testify to the faith and the hope that is within them.

I would like to suggest that if our evangelism, our proclamation of the Gospel, makes little sense to so many people today, it is perhaps because that question is no longer being asked of Christians: "Why do you live the way that you do?" It is not being asked because most people already know the answer to the question. They know that we live the way that we do, by and large, for the same reasons that all those around us live the way that they do: for reasons of class and race and nation—all those

things that make the life of the Church utterly predictable on
mere sociological grounds. It is the predictability of our style of
life that has so damaged the integrity of our proclamation of the
Gospel and so undermined the authority and the power of our
worship. Conversely, it was the power of the style of life, the
way of living, of the earliest Christian communities that gave
their worship such force and gave their evangelism such a compelling kind of authority.

Jesus calls us to what we might call a "breakaway" lifestyle.
He says things such as, "Unless you give away all that you have
you cannot be my disciple." These kinds of remarks might be
referred to as the "hard sayings" of Jesus. It is easy to see why. I
often wonder if he said these things when crowds got too large,
when it became too easy to follow him. One can imagine the
feelings of his disciples—just when things were going well, when
he was really becoming popular, when the people were coming
around, and it really looked as if they might have a mass movement on their hands—after they would hear Jesus say something
like that. Then the poeple would start slowly trailing off, so that
the circle once again would become small.

Why did he say these "hard" things? What do they mean for
us? The hard sayings of Jesus are a continuing challenge to the
complacency and the comfort that is, first, a natural drift of all
of humanity, but is also for us so powerfully reinforced by this
culture. In a nuclear age the fundamental question, politically
and theologically, is the question of security. It is crucial to
understand where our security is and what our security is in. Our
security can be in many things—money, our possessions, roles
that we have for ourselves, our self-images, our relationships,
various forms of status and comfort and protection, power over
others, or even intimacy with others. Yet, wherever it is, it is
important for us to know where our securities are, because all of
our securities can and will be used against us, which is to say all
of our securities can and will be used to control us, to intimidate
us, to restrain us, and to rob us of our freedom in Christ. What
happens is that we hear the Word of God and we move just a bit
further than we have moved before—beyond the places of
comfort and familiarity—but just when we begin to move out

too far, it is as if the world reaches out and hooks us right at the place of our deepest securities and then slowly reels us right back into the circle of control.

It is important to know where our securities are because real change and real renewal will always require sacrifice, and sacrifice requires freedom. There is no change, there is no justice, there is no peace, there is no renewal, without cost. This is true on a personal level, on a corporate level, and certainly on a political level. If there is no change without cost, and no capacity for sacrifice without freedom, then the question is who are the people who can bear the cost of making change possible? Who are the people free enough of the world's securities to make the necessary sacrifices, in other words, who are the people free enough to sacrifice for the things in which they believe?

There is a moral power greater than any other in the world, which comes from standing before the world, free of its securities, free of its rewards and punishments, and therefore free to offer ourselves for what we know to be true and for what we know God is calling us to do. When Jesus stood before Pilate, one could imagine, perhaps, what Pilate was thinking—that this renegade rabbi was not showing the proper respect, that his face did not bear the expected fear and awe to which Pilate was accustomed. In essence, what Pilate then said to Jesus was, "You need to remember, you need to know who I am. I am the symbol of the greatest power on the earth, and I have the power of life and death over you. Your life is in my hands, I have control over you, and you had better understand that. The rewards and punishments that I have to dispense have the whole world controlled, and you had better understand in whose presence you are standing." However, Jesus responded, perhaps shaking his head with a kind of pity for the illusions within which this man was himself trapped, "You have no power over me. You have no power over me, save that which my father has given to you." What Jesus meant was, "I am free, and I am standing here free of your securities and your rewards and your punishments. I am not afraid, I am not intimidated, I am not controlled, I am here to be about the work of my father." Who will have the freedom to stand before the world like that?

The costs of renewal in the Church are going to get higher and higher, and the cost of justice and peace will increase. There are going to be very serious tests of faith facing us in the 1980's. There is a new military consensus abroad in the land that will severely test the faith of those who would be sons and daughters of God by being peacemakers in the world. It is going to mean more and to cost more, I am convinced, simply to name the name of Jesus. So where will we root ourselves and where will our security finally be?

This question of security, which is so intensely a political question, is finally a question of worship. Jesus stood before Pilate as free as he was because he knew who he was, and he knew his life in relationship to his father. His security in being rooted in the love of his father was the source of his political threat to Pilate. Consider what Jesus says about that same kind of security and freedom which he wants for us: "Do not store up for yourselves treasure on earth where it grows rusty and moth-eaten and thieves break in to steal it. Store up treasure in Heaven where there is no moth and no rust to spoil it, no thieves to break in and steal it. For where your wealth is, there will your heart be also." That is not what I hear in the churches. What I hear is, "Where your heart is, that is where your treasure will be." In other words, it is not so much what we have, what we possess, the amount that we own; rather, it is our attitude toward those things. As long as we are free, as long as we are willing to give it all up, then everything is fine. As long as our heart is in the right place, it does not matter how much wealth we possess.

Jesus, however, does not seem to agree with that point of view. He says, on the contrary, "Where your wealth is, that is where your heart is as well." He goes on, "No servant can be slave to two masters, for either he will hate the first and love the second, or he will be devoted to the first and think nothing of the second. You cannot serve God and Mammon." And here Jesus is not simply giving advice. He is not saying you ought not to try to serve God and money. He is not saying it is a good idea not to do it and he would rather you did not. He is saying you simply cannot do it. It is like the law of gravity—it cannot be broken. You cannot serve God and money at the same time. They are rival gods in our lives; they are rival claimants for our time, our energy, and our resources.

Jesus then goes on to give a little teaching, which, every time I read it, strikes me with my own lukewarmness and faithlessness, because he says, "Therefore I bid you put away all anxious thought about food and drink to keep you alive and clothes to cover your body. Surely life is more than food and the body more than clothes. Look at the birds of the air. They neither sow nor reap nor store in barns, yet your heavenly father feeds them. You are worth more than the birds. Is there one among you who by anxious thought can add a foot to his height? And why be anxious about clothes? Consider how the lilies grow in the fields. They do not work, they do not spin, and yet I tell you that Solomon in all of his splendor was not arrayed like one of these. But if that is how God clothes the grass of the fields, which is there tomorrow and thrown in the stove, how then will he not all the more clothe you? How little faith you have. Now do not ask anxiously what we are to eat, what we are to drink, and what we shall wear. All these things are for the heathen to run after, but not for you, because your heavenly father knows that you need them all. Set your mind on God's kingdom and his justice before everything else, and all the rest will come to you as well." We make a mistake if we think that passage merely talks about economics or about social justice. It is a passage about whether or not we can trust God. It is about whether we finally know ourselves to be God's children at such a deep level that we can live according to his way, so that others, the "heathen who are running after all these things," will raise that question anticipated by Peter: "Why is it that you people live the way that you do?"

A scribe once came up to Jesus and said, "Teacher, I'll follow you wherever you go." Now how often do we hear that today in the churches? Jesus replied to him, "Foxes have holes and birds of the air have nests, but the Son of Man has nowhere to lay his head," implying that "If you want to follow, then I want you to follow, but count the cost, and the cost is to trust me."

My own conversion passage is Matthew 25:31-46, the parable of the sheep and the goats at the judgment day. "When the Son of Man comes in his glory and all his angels with him, then he

will sit on his glorious throne and before him will be gathered all
the nations, and he will separate them one from another as a
shepherd separates sheep from goats. And he will place the sheep
at his right hand, but the goats at the left. Then the king will say
to those at his right hand, 'Come, O blessed of my father. Inherit
the kingdom prepared for you from the foundation of the world,
for I was hungry and you gave me food, I was thirsty and you
gave me drink, I was a stranger and you welcomed me, I was
naked and you clothed me, I was sick and you visited me, I was in
prison and you came to see me.' And then the righteous will answer him, 'Lord, when did we see you hungry and feed you, thirsty
and give you drink, when did we see you a stranger and welcome
you, naked and clothe you, when were you sick or in prison?'
And the king will answer them, 'Truly I say to you, as you did it
unto one of the least of these my brethren, you did it to me.'
And then he will say to those on his left, 'Depart from me, you
cursed, into the eternal fire prepared for the Devil and his angels,
for I was hungry and you gave me no food, I was thirsty and you
gave me no drink, I was a stranger and you did not welcome me,
naked and you did not clothe me, sick and in prison and you did
not visit me.' Then they will answer, 'Lord, when did we see you
hungry or thirsty or a stranger or naked or sick or in prison and
did not minister to you?' And he will answer them, 'Truly I say
to you, as you did it not to one of the least of these, you did it
not to me.' And they will go away into eternal punishment, but
the righteous into eternal life.''

Here is the risen and glorified Christ, not just the carpenter of
Nazareth, but the Son of God. Yet, the Son of God, ''in all his
glory,'' is to be found among the suffering and the poor. The
passage says that this is his natural habitation. All of those
gathered before him cried, ''Lord, when did we see you there?''
No one knew where to look for him, but the creator and the
judge of the earth had so cast his lot with the least of the earth
that to serve them was to serve him, and to ignore them and
neglect them and abuse them was to ignore, neglect, and abuse
him. In other words, there is a God whose natural habitation is
among the poor, and who stands among them, asking those who
would name his name not only the question, ''How much do you

love them?'' Jesus stands among the poor, saying to all who would be his followers, ''How much do you love me? And I will know how much you love me by the way that you love them.''

Simple facts: The world's people are poor. The Church in America is rich. We have read all the statistics, so I shall simply mention just one of them: six percent of the world's people consume forty percent of the earth's resources—a twentieth consume almost half. Brothers and sisters, that is not simply bad stewardship. That is theft from the poor, and that is a sin against Christ, if we are to believe the Bible. These simple facts set our context, and it is our most important context.

Pentecostal economics is rooted in that context. In the second chapter of Acts it says that the early Christians devoted themselves to teaching, to fellowship, to the breaking of bread, and to prayer. It says many signs and wonders were done, and it says all that believed were together and had all things in common. They were drawn together by the force of their fellowship, and the message of the passage is that the coming of the Holy Spirit created among those Christians a common life. The fruit of that common life was that they sold all their possessions and goods and distributed them to any and all who had need.

If someone should write a book about all those passages of Scripture upon which the Church has spent the most time and effort to avoid, this passage would be high on the list. The Church has performed endless theological acrobatics to avoid the implications of what the first Christians did when the Holy Spirit invaded their lives. The standard rebuttals are well known: it was simply an experiment, an early model for the Church's life which failed. Not being a people who entertain failure very well, we can safely disregard this and keep our economic lives private. However, it did not simply fail. There is much evidence to support the fact it found expression again and again in the life of the Church, even to the present day.

Others want to find in this passage a new rule for the Church, a new law saying somehow that a common purse is the road to renewal. Somehow, if one simply takes all one's money and throws it in the pot, one will be renewed. I can testify to the fact that that is also not true, nor is it the point of the passage.

The passage is neither a description of failure nor a new rule for the Church's life. The passage is simply a description of what happened when the Holy Spirit invaded the life of the early Christians. The coming of the Spirit among them shattered the old and normal economic assumptions and created an entirely different economic order—a different political economy among them, if you will. It was a new way of thinking and a new way of living, which also affected their relationship to money and to their goods. They shared a common life in which economics was no longer a private matter, but a matter of fellowship, and, in fact, a central question of fellowship. It would not have been possible for the early Christians to have conceived of a way to share all of their lives, to share everything spiritual, and not to share their economic lives. To share their lives meant to share every part of their life together.

Paul, in 2 Corinthians 8, when taking up a collection for the Jerusalem church, which had suffered from famine, goes on to correlate spiritual unity with economic equality. He wants the congregation to understand that the unity of heart and mind, which God wants them to have with their brothers and sisters in Jerusalem, involves, among other things, economic equality among them.

What do these teachings have to say to us in a world in which, not only are most people poor, but where the Church is poor in the places of the world that are poor, and rich in the places that also are rich? It is to say that not only does our way of living crush the poor, but also that our way of living, in a world where other Christians are poor, is a violation of Christian fellowship. Our wealth breaks the solidarity of the body of Christ, and the complete lack of equality among us, the utter disparity between rich and poor, not only in the world but even in the Church, is an offense to the unity of the body of Christ. These early Christians did not share their resources out of obligation or because of a new rule; they shared everything they had out of a tremendous experience of joy and spontaneous offering. They had experienced the Holy Spirit, and their response was to share everything that they had.

This passage in Acts is crucial today in the Church for a number of people, but people who find very different things in the passage. Movements of charismatic renewal find in this passage the centerpiece to all that they are about. Here is the coming of the Spirit at Pentecost, and that is crucial. There are others in the Church concerned with justice and the redistribution of wealth, for whom this passage is also key. Yet, somehow each group manages to miss in the passage what the other group finds. Why does that happen? Why is it that we continue to take part and not the whole? Why do we act again and again out of false choices? According to Acts, the new economy, doing something different about bread, is a visible consequence of the Spirit's presence. It is a sign. It is perhaps even a test of the fullness of the presence of the Spirit. That is a very hard thing to hear for those who would rather stay in the Upper Room with the Spirit, never coming down on the street to live out the new economy that the Spirit has created. Yet, it is the very presence of the Holy Spirit, which breaks down the old assumptions and breaks down our self-interest and makes the new economy possible. For many, however, to talk of the Spirit is an embarrassment. It is awkward, it sounds too much like our pious past and the religious upbringing we want to forget.

The lesson of Acts 2 and 4 is that any spiritual renewal that does not result in a new economy among the believers is incomplete at best and inauthentic at worst. Yet, the message is also that the creation of that new economy in the Church is not going to come through good intentions, through good political analysis, through good preaching, through good educational programs, or through social action projects. It will come about only as we begin to experience what the early Christians experienced in their own lives, when the Spirit invaded them and they discovered a new economy among themselves. The Holy Spirit is the engine of that new economy, and, as such, the Holy Spirit is the greatest threat to the economic system that we and the rest of the world now labor under.

Perhaps the most famous and striking of all the passages about the teaching of Jesus on this subject is when he spoke to the rich young ruler. This story was always one of my favorites, because I could take that story into a wealthy congregation and really lay them out. By the time I would finish, I had succeeded in making them feel so guilty and terrible about themselves, or so guilty or angry—but in either case so absolutely convicted— that I could walk out feeling so damned prophetic, convinced again that I was on the cutting edge.

However, there are two things in that passage, and like things we often miss in the Bible, they have come home to me in recent times and have changed my relationship to that passage. The first thing is that the passage actually says Jesus looked at the young man and that he loved him. I believe that young man knew that day that he had been loved. What that means is that the young ruler had to turn away, not only from one who brought him the meaning of the kingdom in a relationship to his possessions, but also from one who clearly did love him.

The second part of that passage, which also I always seem to pass over, refers to the point at which Jesus says, "Sell all that you have and give it to the poor. . . ." It was there I would stop, as if to say, "Take what you have and sell it to the poor and drop me a line, write me a card sometime, give me a call, and let me know how all of it comes out. Good luck, be on your way, I wish you the best." For people who are trapped, who are under the control of their possessions, who have been taught from their earliest years that their very worth and identity as human beings comes in their possession and consumption of things—for people who have succumbed to the power and who are possessed, like a demon, by the control of this filthy, rotten system—that word is very cruel and very insensitive. However, Jesus did not stop where I had stopped. He said, "Sell all that you have, give it to the poor, *and come and follow me.*"

In the New Testament whenever Jesus says, "Come and follow me," what he is saying is, "I would like to invite you to join my community. Pack up your life, pick up your bag, come live with us. Come share our life, come join us, and come experience a new and different kind of security which we have found." When people trust God together, then we shall find that those people are very much like us—with the same fears, the same problems, the same history—but are also people who are learning together to find a new way of living, and who can help lead others along the way.

If we care about rebuilding the Church, if we care about breaking the stranglehold that this economic system has on the Church's life, it means creating places, it means creating communities. It means creating environments that people can be invited into, where repentance is more than a word, and where a concrete and visible alternative begins to be demonstrated. That is the meaning of the call to repentance as I see Jesus offering it. It is never divorced from the creation of a new people whose life intends to be the first fruit, the pilot project, the seed of that new order which God intends for the whole of the creation.

When Jesus says, "You cannot serve God and Mammon," he is simply saying we have to make a choice. If we are going to serve Mammon, we had really better do it well. If we are going to make Mammon our god, we had better make sure that we are secure in his worship. If we find our loyalty in Mammon, if that is where we are counting for our security, we had better build up some pretty hefty security, because this society is very brutal to those who commit themselves to its assumptions and to its structures without adequately protecting themselves. That is what the insurance companies say, and they are right. However, if we choose another god, another lord, another form of security, then we must choose to reject the security that Mammon offers and look elsewhere for our care.

In conclusion, I would like to relate a piece of commentary I heard recently about the lily in the field. The commentator said, "The lily is taken care of when it is in its proper environment. If you take the lily and put it down here on the carpet it is going to die, because it is not where it belongs. The lily belongs in the field, where God can care for it, and we shall be taken care of, too, in our proper environment." Our proper environment is the community of faith called the Church, an environment of love and support where God can take care of us, because we, like the lily, shall be where we are supposed to be, and shall be under the care of the one who cares so much for us. If all that we mean by renewal does not generate within our congregations the power of community to break free from the hold that Mammon has on the Church's life in this country, there will be no renewal worth talking about. But if we can experience the Holy Spirit in the way the early Christians did, if we can understand Pentecostal economics, if we can trust God, if we can stand with God among the poor; then people are likely to ask of us, "Why do you people live the way that you do?" And then we, listening to Peter, can be ready to give reason for the faith and the hope that is within us.